State Government and Economic Performance

PAUL BRACE

State Government and Economic Performance

THE JOHNS HOPKINS UNIVERSITY PRESS
Baltimore and London

© 1993 The Johns Hopkins University Press
All rights reserved
Printed in the United States of America on acid-free paper

The Johns Hopkins University Press
2715 North Charles Street
Baltimore, Maryland 21218-4319
The Johns Hopkins Press Ltd., London

LIBRARY OF CONGRESS CATALOGING-IN-PUBLICATION DATA

Brace, Paul, 1954–
    State government and economic performance / Paul Brace.
        p.   cm.
    Includes bibliographical references and index.
    ISBN 0-8018-4494-0
    1. Local finance—United States.   2. Finance, Public—United States—States.
3. Intergovernmental fiscal relations—United States.   I. Title.
HJ9145.B73   1993
336'.01473—dc20   92-24177

A catalog record for this book is available from the British Library.

For K.J.B.

CONTENTS

List of Figures   ix

List of Tables   xi

Preface   xiii

1. The Mystery of State Political Economy   1
2. National Context and State Capacity   16
3. The Political Economy of Dependence in Arizona and Texas   33
4. The Political Economy of Intervention in Michigan and New York   51
5. Context: Isolating the Economies of States   66
6. Capacity: The Impact of State Government, Party, and Policy on State Economic Performance   87
7. Conclusions: The States and Their Economies in Context   113

Appendix A: Data and Measurement   125

Appendix B: Methodology   128

Notes   131

Index   147

FIGURES

1. State vs. National Variation: Annual Change in Per Capita Personal Income, 1968–1989   81
2. Dispersion in Per Capita Personal Income, 1968–1989   82
3. State vs. National Variation: Annual Change in Nonagricultural Employment, 1968–1989   83
4. Dispersion in Nonagricultural Employment, 1968–1989   83
5. State vs. National Variation: Annual Change in Value Added by Manufacturing, 1968–1987   85
6. Dispersion in Value Added by Manufacturing, 1968–1987   85
7. Governor's Power in Four States   89
8. Amounts Spent per Legislator on Legislative Operations in Four States, 1967–1988   90
9. Financial Assistance Policies in Four States and the Nation   91
10. Tax Incentives in Four States and the Nation   92
11. Policies Providing Special Services for Industry in Four States and the Nation   92
12. Per Capita Tax Revenues in Four States, 1967–1986   93
13. Investment Expenditures in Four States, 1967–1989   94
14. Per Capita Value of Mineral Resources in Four States, 1967–1984   96
15. Labor Union Membership in Four States, 1968–1985   98
16. Per Capita Defense Expenditures in Four States, 1968–1989   98
17. A New American Political Economy?   110

TABLES

1. State Economic Intervention as a Zero-sum Game   12

2. State Capacity and National Context   31

3. Classification of States according to Growth Rates and National Influence   69

4. Annual Change in Per Capita Income by State, 1968–1989: The Effects of the National Economy and State Trends   71

5. Personal Income: Classification of States according to Responsiveness to the National Economy and State-Level Economic Trends   72

6. Annual Change in Nonagricultural Employment by State, 1968–1989: The Effects of the National Economy and State Trends   74

7. Nonagricultural Employment: Classification of States according to Responsiveness to the National Economy and State-Level Economic Trends   75

8. Annual Change in Value Added by Manufacturing by State, 1968–1987: The Effects of the National Economy and State Trends   77

9. Value Added by Manufacturing: Classification of States according to Responsiveness to the National Economy and State-Level Economic Trends   78

10. Pooled Analysis of the Growth in Per Capita Personal Income, 1968–1982   101

11. Pooled Analysis of the Growth in Per Capita Personal Income, 1983–1989   104

12. Pooled Analysis of Growth in Nonagricultural Employment, 1968–1982   105
13. Pooled Analysis of Growth in Nonagricultural Employment, 1983–1989   106
14. Pooled Analysis of Growth in Value Added by Manufacturing, 1968–1982   108
15. Pooled Analysis of Growth in Value Added by Manufacturing, 1983–1987   109

This book was motivated by a desire to solve an enigma involving the role of the American states in shaping their economic performance. We have an abundance of contradictory theoretical propositions about the impact of government and policy on economic performance, yet we have virtually no evidence that state-level efforts have had any positive effects on their economies. While this enigma holds an intellectual attraction in its own right, it has become an issue of increasing practical concern in the last two decades as state politicians across the land have placed unprecedented emphasis on stimulating the economies of their states. Unfortunately, no one can say what works, what fails, or why.

If the interplay of political and economic forces in the states was clear or obvious, a book such as this would be unnecessary. To unravel this complexity and to make some sense out of the myriad of conflicting theoretical propositions and contradictory empirical findings, this study examines the history of the states generally as well as the contemporary experiences of selected states in detail to develop a picture of the forces affecting the economies of the states and their political responses to their economies. State-level political-economic dramas, it will be seen, are played out on a stage shaped largely by the nation's economic performance and are highly dependent on the national economy. Of course, the reach of the nation's economy varies over time and dependence on that economy varies across states. Government and economic performance in the states, in essence, is a puzzle nested within the larger national economy. We may understand the political economies of states, their possibilities, and their limits when they are viewed within their proper context.

It is hard to pinpoint the exact origins of this book. Like most people, I have watched the dramatic economic ups and downs of the American states. I resided in Michigan in the early 1980s during a crisis surpassed in this century only by the Great Depression. Eventually, I ended up in Colorado, ostensibly a growth state. While there, two events occurred that stimulated my thinking about states and their economies. The first was the publication of Mancur Olson's intriguing book, *The Rise and Decline of Nations*.[1] The second was my experience derived from observing the Colorado General Assembly. I, like many others, was impressed by Olson's argument that newer states were less hampered by the ossifying effects of groups. Yet, in observing the operations of the Colorado General Assembly firsthand, I was struck by how powerful selected groups were in winning their way in this comparatively new state. Furthermore, I found that while many in the legislature would promote conditions that were supposedly ripe for business, these conditions did not help the state through the middle of the 1980s; Colorado had few resources at its disposal to combat an economic downturn. From observing the operations of this amateurish legislature, I became interested in the role that political institutions might play in the process of economic development.

From these beginnings I sought to understand better how institutional development might relate to Olson's argument. My essay "The Political Economy of Collective Action"[2] guided the consideration of political capacity discussed in chapters 2 and 6. I also explored the effects of the national economy on the economic performance of the states in "Isolating the Economies of States" and "The Changing Context of State Political Economy."[3] These articles and collaborative work with Youssef Cohen, Robert Dudley, and Gary Mucciaroni helped shape chapters 5 and 6.[4]

This book has benefited tremendously from collegial input from many helpful scholars along the way. Gary King nudged me to the appropriate methodology for the questions I was addressing and provided helpful comments in the early stages. I had the opportunity to meet Mancur Olson during his visit to New York University in 1988 and later that year served on a panel with him at the American Political Science Association. Each of these meetings provoked my thinking. Conference participation or other communications with Virginia Gray, Bryan Jones, William Keech, Margery Ambrosius, and David Lowery also helped to focus and refine my argument. Youssef Cohen provided many useful comments about comparative inquiry. Extended discussions with Gary Mucciaroni made me continuously aware of the two sides to every argument. Barbara Hinckley gave generous amounts of her time and willingly read many drafts, providing penetrating comments and much-needed guidance in the preparation of the book. Through this and many other endeavors Melinda Gann Hall has been a great friend and colleague, providing support, advice, and a receptive ear.

The Institute of Government and Public Affairs of the University of Illinois is an excellent environment in which to work and I owe its director, Robert Rich, and its associate directors, Paul Quirk and Will White, a tremendous debt of gratitude for their encouragement and the support they made available. I am also indebted to my colleagues in the Department of Political Science for their forbearance and understanding during the completion of this manuscript. Henry Y. K. Tom, of the Johns Hopkins University Press, was most helpful in the preparation of this book. Through the review process, the manuscript was strengthened in style and content.

Finally, I would like to thank my wife, Klaudia, for her support, extraordinary patience, and uncommon sense of humor.

State Goverment and Economic Performance

CHAPTER 1

The Mystery of State Political Economy

A visitor to any state capitol today would be impressed by how politicians and those trying to influence state policy believe that government action can enhance or hinder state economic prosperity. As noted in recent accounts, growth management has become a top priority of state lawmakers.[1] Politicians and groups devote tremendous energy to debating the possible economic consequences of a tax or program on a state's economy. Lawmakers, lobbyists, and bureaucrats evaluate policies in terms of their likely effects on state business climates and employment. Yet while these extensive and sometimes heated activities take place, we have almost no evidence that state governments have *any* effect at all on their economies. The mystery of state political economy has taken on new importance in recent years due to dramatic changes in the American states over the course of the last several decades. For most of the post–World War II era it was up to the national government to manage the economy; since the 1970s, however, the states have become increasingly involved in their economies. The causes and consequences of this change are the fundamental focus of this book.

Several important signals suggest that the American economy is undergoing a significant transformation. The changing structure of American production and the increasing challenge of international competition have created new pressures for state officials. The nature and extent of the national recession of the late 1970s and early 1980s placed additional stress on state governments. Increasingly, they have had to fill voids in the evolving American economy. Adding to these pressures were changing policy initiatives during the Reagan Administration that reduced the involvement of the federal government

in the private economy. Federal budget deficits during the 1980s reduced the amount of federal dollars available for domestic programs
and placed added demands on state governments.

A noteworthy feature of the new economy is the reversal of a
longstanding trend in growth in per capita personal income. Throughout this century disparities in per capita income among the states grew
smaller and smaller.[2] These disparities diminished from the early 1930s
to the late 1970s as per capita incomes rose faster in low-income states
than high-income states. Poorer states, often from the South and the
West, were catching up with their more developed counterparts in
the Northeast and Midwest. Since 1978 this fifty-year trend has re-
versed.

The expansive role of the federal government through the 1960s
and the dominance of the American economy in many of the world's
markets may have acted like a rising tide that lifted all boats. At the
state level much could be left to chance and economic growth would
still occur. Production practices and technology would disperse to
formerly less developed states, stimulating rapid economic growth.
Owing to past underdevelopment, these states possessed attractive
advantages that served to stimulate their economic growth without
active economic intervention. Few states were emphasizing economic
development in this era.

New politics in Washington have ushered in a new environment
for the states. Some have argued that there is a cyclicality in the roles
of the American state governments.[3] In conservative periods, the role
of state governments has expanded; in liberal or programmatic periods
the role of the national government has expanded. The Reagan years
fostered political conservatism at the national level and the Reagan
policies to cut federal grants and rely more heavily on the states have
made their mark. Increasingly the American states have had to shoul-
der greater fiscal and programmatic burdens.[4]

Luckily, the states were preparing for this long before it hit. Since
the 1960s most American states have been modernizing their governments in one way or another. Many states reformed and empowered
their political institutions, giving them greater capacity to address
public concerns.[5] Where often state governments had been amateurish
and chaotic coming into the 1960s, by the mid 1980s the Advisory
Commission on Intergovernmental Relations could report that "state
governments have [been] transformed in almost every facet of their
structure and operations."[6]

In the changing political-economic context of the 1980s, many states
experienced significant reversals in their economic fortunes. Part of
this may be the result of the changed role of the federal government.

Where once the U.S. economy was "nationalizing," with growth extending to almost all states, development in poorer states slowed and politically and economically advanced states experienced heightened growth during the 1980s. During this period, many rich states got richer while poorer states fell behind.[7] Typically, states that had experienced awesome economic growth in the 1960s and 1970s, often with limited government capacity and minimal government intervention in their economies, were now suffering stagnation; states with extensive traditions of government intervention displayed heightened economic growth. These developments have challenged many conventional interpretations of the role of state government in state economies.

A primary concern of this book is the comparative ability of state governments to cope with this new economic environment. Specifically, the book asks what effect, if any, state governments, policies, and parties have on state economic performance over time. Issues embodied in this question are of obvious importance to students of the American states and to policymakers in states trying to cope with this new environment. These issues, however, are of even broader concern because they strike at the heart of some central theoretical issues in political economy. Economic and political theorists have provided an abundance of theories arguing either that government is a hindrance to prosperity, or that government is essential to prosperity. Yet while we have a wealth of interesting theoretical propositions about the economic consequences of government and policy, we have a perilous scarcity of comparative systematic evaluation of the role government and policy play in economic performance, or empirical support for these propositions.

A note of caution is warranted at the outset. States have open economies with labor and capital moving freely from state to state. Consequently the states are highly responsive to forces outside their control, which contributes to the elusive nature of economic development. In a recent study of selected states and their economies, David Osborne argues that economic development is not a thing but a process.[8] Although he identifies many ingredients present in growing economies, in the end he believes the process to be "capricious and unpredictable."[9] David Lampe presents a similar observation in his intensive examination of economic recovery in Massachusetts, contending that "no individual or organization from business, academe, or government can claim credit for consciously engineering [the recovery]. It happened by itself, fostered by a remarkable combination of favorable conditions that emerged from the particular culture of the region and by chance."[10] Conclusions such as these by observers close to the topic of state political economy underscore the mysterious nature of the process of state political economy.

The conclusion that economic development is capricious and occurs by chance is unsettling. First, it suggests that it is not possible to understand why some states grow more rapidly than others. Second, it indicates that government or policy has no systematic role in economic development. Third, this further indicates that the changing focus of state governments and their increasing efforts at promoting economic growth have no tangible impact. Intellectually and practically speaking none of these conclusions is palatable. It is the premise of this book that state economic growth, while made complex by the openness of state economies, is nonetheless a phenomenon that may be unraveled; an additional premise is that the effects of state government and policy in this process of economic change may be isolated and understood.

Government and the Economy in Theory

The appropriate beginning for a study of the role of state governments in their economies is a brief survey of theory concerning the general effects of government in shaping economic performance. The observations of Adam Smith are an obvious starting point for any discussion of government and economic performance.[11] Smith's major contribution was a description of how the pursuit of individual self-interest in commerce resulted in collective prosperity for society. Yet, Smith allowed a role for government but was not explicit about its proper limits. According to Smith, market exchanges are based on price mechanisms and thus there is no need for central planning or directing authority. Also, price mechanisms contribute to the social order and allow rapid changes in the allocation of resources and production of goods according to market signals. Smith argued that despite the lack of central coordination, the outcome of market transactions was mutually beneficial and this could not be achieved by a bureaucratic authority charged with achieving the same end.

Smith did realize that the voluntary market system required some government activity. First, a set of rules, a legal framework, upheld by the state that facilitates the operation of market exchanges. In particular, property rights must be guaranteed by the legal system. Second, Smith ascribed the role of national defense to the state. Third, Smith realized the state would need to produce some public goods that the market would fail to produce.

Debates about the proper role for government have concerned the desirability and effects of legal frameworks and public goods. Political economic theories about the effects of government and public policy fall neatly into two camps. One camp extols the virtues of the unfettered market and underscores the inefficiencies and market distortions that arise from government interference. The other camp points to the allocational shortcomings of the market and stresses the need for government to stimulate the demand necessary to promote economic growth. These perspectives will be explored briefly below.

MARKET-ORIENTED APPROACHES

Although its roots may be traced to much earlier, the 1870s are usually considered the origin of neoclassical economics.[12] A central feature of neoclassical interpretations of the economy was that free markets were stable and self-correcting. Market-oriented approaches to economic development have shared this belief. Development results from market efficiencies and economic growth. Efficient employment of resources means that no reallocation could increase the total value of goods and services in a society. Growth is an increase in the magnitude of the total per capita product. From this perspective government is not only irrelevant in the development process, it may impede it.

Hayek's studies are of enormous importance to proponents of market economics. His works articulate the liberal principles of individualism, a constitutionally limited role for the state, and faith in the market. Much of Hayek's work has been an attack on the postwar trends toward state intervention in the economy or in welfare activities.[13] His "spontaneous order" or "catallaxy" are the modern counterpart of Smith's "invisible hand." Hayek believed that inequality was a necessary element while attaining progress. Incentives are necessary for this process to operate effectively.

Like Hayek, Milton Friedman is an ardent opponent of government intervention. In *Capitalism and Freedom* he argued that government activity should protect us from our enemies, preserve law and order, enforce private contracts, and foster competitive markets.[14] More recently Friedman has reasserted the value of markets by examining cases of government inefficiency and the damaging economic effects of well-intended government policies.[15]

Obviously, neoclassical economists view government intervention critically. On one level, they stress the impracticality of state activity. While government actions may produce some distributional gains, they also will contribute to inefficiencies. Since government lacks ways to estimate the unintended economic consequences of public policies, state economic intervention is a risky proposition. On another level, neoclassical economists have emphasized the political realities of formulating public policies. One writer notes that neoclassical economists believe that the state, far from being "an exogenous force, trying to do good, is at least partly endogenous and the policies it institutes will reflect vested interests in society."[16]

Influential studies by Buchanan and others in the public choice tradition shift attention to interactions and institutions outside and beyond the confined competitive market process, while applying essentially the same tools as those used in interactions within the process.[17] The essential feature of many political activities is that while they are rational and not wasteful from a private viewpoint they are often socially wasteful. So, if political allocation is to be undertaken without causing rent-seeking, then such allocation has to be done without creating differential advantage to some groups and, more important, a credible commitment not to depart in the future from such an allocation procedure has to be given. Government, composed of self-interested politicians, will inevitably produce policies that distort market outcomes thereby causing societal inefficiencies.

Working from economic concepts (i.e., rational, utility maximizing activity), Mancur Olson has analyzed the economic consequences of political activity and explored the consequences of collective action for the economic performance of states and nations in *The Rise and Decline of Nations* (1982). In earlier work, Olson forcefully argued that there were biases in the ability of groups to form.[18] Some groups, either small or with access to selective incentives, would form while potential large groups faced serious impediments and would not form. Over time, certain interests in society would be overrepresented while others would not be represented at all, contributing to economic stagnation. As well-organized distributional coalitions, essentially interest groups, acquire benefits for their members—a process which diverts societal resources away from more productive use—these exclusive distributional coalitions become more widespread and effective, suffocating the market economy. In the long run collective action reduces the economic output of a society as more and more resources are diverted to organizationally advantaged groups and away from market allocation. Hence the political success of certain interests can undermine the economic health of a state or nation.

Criticisms of the Market-Oriented Economics. Approaches that extol the virtues of the unfettered market are seldom aware of the important role that government has played in facilitating market transactions. One critic of Hayek notes that, while accurately targeting several political economic problems, Hayek "fails to realize that the politics he abhors is in large part a product of the economic order he defends. The same motives that drive people to seek their advantage in the market encourage them to pursue their end by political means as well. Self-interest, that great engine of material progress, teaches us to respect results not principles."[19] T. N. Srinivasan points out another shortcoming of the neoclassical approach: "A curious facet of the neoclassical gem is that it is 'institution free' in that it does not explicitly refer to any state."[20] All too often neoclassical approaches to political economy disdain political outcomes without fully evaluating political processes and institutions.

Clearly, the state has contributed substantially to economic development. As Polanyi observed,

> The road to the free market was kept open by an enormous increase in continuous, centrally organized and controlled interventionism. To make Adam Smith's "simple and natural liberty" compatible with the needs of a human society was a most complicated affair. . . . Just as, contrary to expectation, the invention of labor saving machinery had not diminished but actually increased the uses of human labor, the introduction of free markets, far from doing away with the need for control, regulation, and intervention, enormously increased their range. Administrators had to be constantly on the watch to ensure the free working of the system. Thus even those who wished most ardently to free the state from all unnecessary duties, and whose whole philosophy demanded the restriction of state activities, could not entrust the self-same state with the new powers, organs, and instruments required for the establishment of laissez-faire.[21]

Hodgson comments that "it requires a continuous process of legislation to minimize anomalies and keep the system up to date with a continuously changing social and economic reality."[22] The general point of writers such as Hodgson and Polanyi is that the very existence of a laissez-faire market order, which neoclassical theorists argue is socially most desirable, necessitates the existence of a state that intervenes to promote and facilitate this desired order. It is state policy and institutions that create the necessary framework for the successful flourishing of the free market.

Olson's thesis suffers many similar problems. First, as Dean has noted, Olson ignores the important role that constitutions play in shaping the nature of political conflict.[23] While Olson does acknowledge the intervening influence of political parties, in many ways his argument is "institution free." In addition, Olson's argument that groups become more powerful over time stands in contrast to much of the empirical work in the state politics field that has observed the power of groups diminishes in states as other groups form. In fact, states become more pluralistic, which reduces the power of any single group, or set of groups, to dominate the policy process.[24] Similarly, Olson's thesis ignores the typical evolution of important political institutions that could be expected to modify the influence of groups. As states age, they have developed more powerful governorships and more professionalized legislatures. These institutions can serve to modify group influence and promote more encompassing public policies.

GOVERNMENT INTERVENTION

Mercantilism was the dominant economic theory at the time of the American Revolution. It underscored the importance of government in directing and coordinating societal resources to nurture economic development. The modern counterpart of mercantilism is Keynesianism. The writings of John Maynard Keynes are the typical starting point for contemporary theories of political economy that emphasize the importance of government activity for stimulating economic performance.[25]

Keynes focused on the behavior of the economy as a whole. He believed the signals (in terms of supply and demand) produced by market forces to be sufficient for microeconomic activity to proceed smoothly if aggregate effective demand was properly sustained. Unfortunately, markets do not ensure effective demand as prices and wages could each follow themselves down to disastrously low levels. Ensuring aggregate demand was the lot of government. For aggregate demand to be sustained it is necessary for full employment, or a close approximation, to be maintained. The government does this by providing the necessary fiscal stimuli by way of government spending. The budget becomes a key weapon in economic policy. Abandoning nineteenth-century ideas of balanced budgets, the taxing and spending power of government is used to offset business cycles and their effects on employment, prices, and production levels.

On a practical level, a notable feature of Keynesianism is that the government could pursue its economic policies within a private economy without dramatically altering the state or the basic economy. The United States and Western European nations adopted forms of Keynesian policy in the post–World War II era. Yet, by the late 1960s and certainly the early 1970s Keynesian economics came to be severely criticized. Critics argued that the framework no longer offered successful policy solutions for macroeconomic problems. Stagflation contradicted the Phillips curve. Some have noted that Keynes did not consider his ideas with regard to modern democracy where, as Buchanan and Wagner note, "government is tempted to yield to group pressures to retain or return to power."[26] Still, Therborn observes that the advanced industrial economies that were best able to minimize the detrimental economic consequences of the 1970s were those most committed to Keynesian policies, reflected in an institutionalized commitment to full employment. Austria, Japan, Norway, Sweden, and Switzerland all fit this pattern.[27]

Criticisms of Government Intervention. Some fundamental arguments against government intervention were developed in the discussion of market-oriented approaches to the economy. Yet, beyond these issues, government intervention fell under increasing criticism during the 1970s in the wake of rampant inflation and high levels of unemployment. By the 1980s many came to question the value of government attempts to stabilize the economy.[28]

Additional criticisms of economic intervention would appear to be applicable to the states. First, states have very limited means by which to intervene in their economies. With only very few exceptions, states must balance their budgets. Second, states have no control over their money supply and can hardly be reasoned to have a substantial influence on inflation. At best, government intervention at the state level could be expected to exert a very subtle influence, if any at all.

Government and the Economy in Practice

The actual interplay of politics and economics fits neither neoclassical nor interventionist models well. First, political processes often promote rather than hinder growth. Part of this may be due to what Lindblom calls "the privileged position of business."[29] Given their organizational advantages and latitude of action, business interests have significant advantages over other groups; they may use their political resources to promote rather than hinder growth through the political arena.[30] Furthermore, political entrepreneurs are often amenable to proposals that may promote economic growth. Bryan Jones and Lynn Bachelor note that politicians are open to influence from the business community and argue that "through the public powers to tax and to incur debt, governments use the productive capacity of the private economy to generate the resources necessary to produce public services."[31] Hence, contrary to the implications of many market-oriented arguments, government does not necessarily stand as a barrier to growth but may act to promote prosperity for political reasons.

Second, while states or other subnational units may act to promote growth, it is unlikely that they can act in the deliberate and calculated manner required by most interventionist strategies. In his analysis of city politics, John Mollenkopf observed that few of the political actors were aware of the systemic consequences of their actions. When they were, it was the political consequences that weighed most heavily. The result was a "jumbled" progrowth programmatic framework that accommodated and logrolled many different interests. Mollenkopf also remarked that subnational politics is governed by a structural logic that shapes political power and government capacity, and contributes to inherently regressive tendencies.[32]

Third, the structural context of subnational units places them in a decidedly different operating environment than central governments. Too often, arguments concerning the appropriate strategies of state or local governments borrow directly from major economic theories such as the market-oriented or interventionist strategies that were originally targeted at nations. These arguments treat states as if they were autonomous economic entities. Yet, as Paul Peterson has argued, local governments exist in a dramatically different context than nation-states.[33] One of the most notable differences of state political economy is its highly permeable character. Nations can isolate themselves from many of the economic and social forces in their environment in ways not available to states or cities. For example, nations can control immigration and thus restrict tides of populations from poorer nations descending upon them. In addition, nations can apply tariffs and quotas and adjust their national currencies in efforts to isolate their economies from external influences. Peterson believes that all except the smallest of nations have economies that are less permeable than local economies. This openness, of course, has particular relevance for the study of states and economic development because exogenous forces may overwhelm local action. States cannot be studied as if they are autonomous economic entities, isolated from national and international economic forces. To understand states and their economies we must consider their economies within a context of largely uncontrollable but important external forces.

Fourth, there are grounds to question the long-term economic value of state economic intervention. Federalism and the mobility of capital and labor place severe limits on the effectiveness of state economic intervention. Charles Tiebout provides a framework that alerts us to the effects of mobility on the provision of public goods. Tiebout's objective was to think of a way of achieving efficient public-goods provision and to characterize the conditions under which it would work. In essence, Tiebout reasoned, the provision of public goods may be responsive to citizen preferences even if the ballot is largely ineffective because citizens may vote with their feet.[34]

One factor individuals consider in choosing the community in which they reside is the tax and service package. Residential mobility is believed to be responsive to the tax burden a resident will bear and the benefits from public services a resident will enjoy. If there are many localities, each with a different tax-service package, individuals will select the ones that give them the greatest satisfaction, presumably the ones that are closest to their desired level of taxation and service. In essence, individuals "shop" among localities and "buy" the one best for them. So, individuals can choose what they want in the public sector and need not compromise through voting.

While Tiebout's thesis directs attention to the efficiency-inducing effects of mobility, it ignores what could be reasoned to be the sub-optimal consequences of mobility. While mobility may induce effi-ciency in the provision of public goods, it also shows that this mobility places governments under extraordinary pressure not to raise taxes or engage in spending. States exist in an environment characterized by a high degree of lateral competition with other states which in many ways is like the traditional prisoner's dilemma. In that well known zero-sum game, two prisoners following their individual self-interest pursue choices that are suboptimal for each. Specifically, each prisoner, held in isolation, implicates the other, resulting in maximum sentences for each. They do not remain silent, the optimal strategy, because of the incentives available to each decision-maker.

States may find themselves in situations analogous to the two pris-oners when it comes to active intervention in their economies for such things as technological development and education and training. As-sume that states must tax or otherwise sacrifice to support such in-tervention. Assume further that state politicians are under pressure not to raise taxes or take resources from other programs. Finally, assume that because of the mobility of capital, labor, and technology between states, many of the benefits of such intervention may be transferred to other states. The strategic problem for states may reduce to the information in Table 1. While intervention by each state (out-come 1) might produce superior economic performance, acting in-dependently the strategy of a given state leads them to avoid inter-vention (option 2) while hoping the other state will intervene (outcomes 2 and 3). Clearly, every state would like a "free ride" on the intervention of others. Unfortunately, following these strategies neither intervenes and their aggregate productivity suffers because of this (outcome 4).

Some have argued that interstate competition between states is not analogous to a zero-sum game. Timothy Bartik, for example, argues that state and local economic development policy has positive benefits

TABLE 1. State Economic Intervention as a Zero-sum Game

		State A	
		Option 1: Raise Taxes for Intervention	Option 2: Do Not Raise Taxes for Intervention
State B	Option 1: Raise Taxes for Intervention	*Outcome 1: Economic Intervention by Each*	*Outcome 2: Intervention by State B, Spillover Benefits for A*
	Option 2: Do Not Raise Taxes for Intervention	*Outcome 3: Intervention by State A, Spillover Benefits for B*	*Outcome 4: No Economic Intervention*

because it may increase productivity and stimulate employment at the national level.[35] National benefits, however, would be unlikely to counteract the forces against intervention operating in states. It would be hard to imagine a state politician announcing their support for a state tax increase to promote state research that would have national economic benefits (although I am sure politicians in neighboring states would applaud loudly).

One way out of the dilemma is through cooperation between states. Unlike the prisoners mentioned above, the states play this game over and over and may learn the consequences of uncooperative behavior. In a renowned study Robert Axelrod demonstrated that cooperation is a dominant strategy in such a situation.[36] Certainly regional alliances and governors' conferences show signs of interjurisdictional cooperation. Despite this, however, some states continue to slash taxes in efforts to lure producers (and their technologies) from more interventionist states, as will be shown later. In the end it is probably safest to conclude that while national and international economic conditions may work to promote cooperative behavior among some or even many states, other states will continue to find it to their advantage not to cooperate. These latter states will promote growth by offering a cheaper environment to producers, thus seeking to capture positive externalities generated by the intervention of other states. As long as noncooperation remains a viable strategy for some states, it is likely that cooperative arrangements will be unstable and intervention by states will rest on a precarious foundation.

Clearly, given these restraints, states are under enormous competitive pressure that gives them little latitude in the area of positive economic intervention. As Ronald Fisher notes,

Spatial externalities are the reason for the general prescription that redistribution and stabilization policy can best be carried out by a central federal government. Expansionary fiscal policy by a state government to increase consumption, for instance, would generate benefits in other jurisdictions where the consumer goods are produced. The state's residents would underestimate the benefits of that action and therefore fail to engage in an efficient amount of stabilization policy. Similarly, a state government is unable to internalize all the costs and benefits of an income-redistribution policy. The mobility of consumers and openness of subnational government economies create the spillovers that limit subnational government effectiveness in these areas.[37]

Thus while states may engage more aggressively in their economies, lateral competition with other states and spatial externalities would appear to serve as very real limits for state activity, limits that are much less acute at the national level. Given these inherent limits, states cannot behave like nations, nor can they intervene as aggressively in their economies as a nation might. Bordering states, pursuing a "beggar thy neighbor" approach to economic growth with low taxes and limited intervention, could reap many of the benefits of their neighbor's prosperity by luring producers and adopting technology and production practices developed by their interventionist neighbor. We may assume that this would induce the interventionist state to adjust its efforts downward. States might not provide adequate physical infrastructure, or support education and technological development, out of fear of losing employers. This process, ultimately, could emphasize being cheap over being good, and technology and the quality of employment in the states could suffer.

The States and Their Economies

It is clear that existing economic theory provides differing expectations about the general influence of government in the economy. Depending on one's ideological predispositions and tastes in economic theories, it could be concluded that the American states should retreat from intervening in their economies or, alternatively, that they should actively pursue policies to stimulate economic growth. Even more problematic than these mixed signals from the theoretical literature are the confusing messages that close observation of the efforts of states in their economies has provided suggesting that the process is capricious. In combination, knowledge about the consequences of state activity on state economic performance is virtually nonexistent.

In the chapters that follow, this situation will be rectified. An examination of American political history will reveal that there have been not one but three political economic eras in the United States. In each of these eras the states have assumed different postures with regard to their economies. Furthermore, these postures have been dictated by the economic context in which they have existed and, more than anything else, this context has been structured by the level of activity of the federal government. An examination of history thus suggests that state effort and consequence has been, and continues to be, conditioned by the national political-economic context. Building from a brief survey of American political-economic history a simple framework for the study of state political economy is presented that points to the importance of state capacity for economic intervention. This importance is contingent, however, on federal economic intervention and national economic conditions.

The heightened economic activism in the states is remarkable given the past experiences of several states. Many of the states that have grown most rapidly in the post–World War II era also appeared to do the least to stimulate their growth programmatically. Alternatively, interventionist states were among the slower growing states in this era. To understand the role of state intervention and its consequences, it is imperative that these anomalies be explored. Often, economic and political change is quite subtle and could escape notice, making it difficult to gauge what role, if any, government and policy played in shaping economic performance. Some states, however, have approached economic development in notably different ways and have undergone dramatic changes in the post–World War II years. If the economic role of state government and policy is to reveal itself, it is most likely to be seen in these dynamic cases. Thus, brief examination of states experiencing rapid growth and states in severe decline can be useful in highlighting key features in the interplay of government and economics during economic change.

Four states—Arizona, Michigan, New York, and Texas—were selected to emphasize distinct dimensions. In addition to their regional diversity, these states differ dramatically in their histories and their economies. Michigan and New York are older states with more diversified economies that began experiencing economic stagnation in the early 1970s. Arizona and Texas are quintessential Sunbelt states with comparatively less developed economies that experienced phenomenal growth in the 1970s. In addition to the fundamental differences in the nature and performance of their economies, these states differ also in politics, displaying significant diversity in ideology,[38] partisanship,[39] and policymaking.[40] Close inspection of the diverse developmental experiences of these four states will illustrate the more salient dimensions of state political economy and how these states have coped with growth and decline. As subsequent chapters will reveal, a successful state strategy in one context can be disastrous in another.

CHAPTER 2

National Context and State Capacity

There are cycles in American history that affect state and national economies. Hence while the states must be seen in a national economic context, the context itself is a shifting one. A. O. Hirschman points to societal swings between private and public interest driven by oscillating disappointments in private and public provision.[1] He reasons that these cycles are perpetuated by alternating periods of conservatism and liberalism. In conservative periods the federal government has been restrained and state governments have taken on many additional responsibilities. In liberal periods the states have taken a back seat as the national government assumed a more active role.

Economists have observed long waves or cycles that characterize patterns of economic growth among the regions of the United States. In some eras, states which are politically and economically less developed experience surges in economic growth. In other eras these states are isolated from economic prosperity centered in more developed parts of the nation.[2] Over the course of American history, the states have existed in dramatically dissimilar economic settings. These disparate contexts have stimulated alternative state responses and, we may presume, have led to differential consequences in terms of economic performance.

The Historical Context of Economic Growth

THE EARLY NINETEENTH CENTURY

National Political-Economic Conditions. The United States emerged from a war that was fought to reject many of the key features of European governance. The characteristic economic philosophy in Western Europe in the eighteenth century was mercantilism, which emphasized the use of state action to promote commerce and industry. By the time of the revolution the American colonies were accustomed to intervention in their economies by government. Despite rejecting the centralized forms of authority practiced in Europe, the new nation was not willing to abandon government's role in nurturing and sustaining economic development.

The Articles of Confederation concentrated governing authority in the separate states, which prevented any effective concentration of power at the national level but also inhibited institutional specialization and contributed to an unstable economic and political environment.[3] The Constitution that followed placed greater authority in a new national government, but distributed it among three separate branches of government. These checked and balanced national powers prevented domination by any single national political institution. Guaranteeing certain powers to the states, federalism checked the penetration of national power by ensuring the integrity of the states. The result of the Constitution was "a serviceable but unassuming national government" with a broad diffusion of power to the states.[4] The role of the federal government in this era was largely to provide services: land offices, post offices, and customs houses were the most notable examples of federal activity.

A larger role for the national government had been articulated by Alexander Hamilton. In his *Report on Manufactures*, Hamilton noted that Americans had "a certain fermentation of mind, a certain activity of speculation and enterprise which if properly directed may be made subservient to useful purposes; but which if left entirely to itself, may be attended with pernicious effects."[5] Hamilton argued for a strong role for the national government as an instrument to mobilize law, technology, and corporate organization to promote the economic development of the new nation. He also believed that governmental expenditures could be used to promote economic growth. His successor as Secretary of the Treasury, Albert Gallatin, envisioned an important role for the national government in constructing infrastructure.[6] With funds from the sale of lands in the territory of Ohio, he started to build the Cumberland Road and the National Turnpike. At the end of Jefferson's Administration Gallatin presented a report detailing an elaborate ten-year plan for internal improvements. The plan called for $20 million of expenditures by the federal government for highway and canal construction. However, a lack of consensus reflecting state and sectoral rivalries at the federal level prevented the Gallatin plan from being implemented.

The presidency of Andrew Jackson saw the explicit rejection of national intervention for purposes of economic development. He vetoed legislation that called for the national government to buy stock in a company that was building a road in Kentucky. Jackson was more opposed to business in government than he was government in business but the effects were the same in terms of state intervention in the economy.[7] Jackson and his supporters believed that voting down internal improvements meant helping the common citizen because government expenditure took money out of the private economy.[8] Until the Civil War the federal government remained very small, with spending barely keeping up with population increases.[9] As noted in one account, federal expenditures in the antebellum period "made little or no contribution to the level of living," with "only a minor portion of Civil and miscellaneous expenditures . . . for developmental purposes."[10]

State Economic Intervention. From colonial times through much of the early nineteenth century, state and local political institutions played a large role in shaping American economic development.[11] While market dysfunctions such as price gouging or shoddy products were the targets of many of these efforts, considerable state governmental energy also went into trying to stimulate economic growth. As one historian comments, "If one includes all the activities of government, and takes into reckoning all the costs, one must conclude that an economic policy, aimed primarily at encouraging the internal growth of the nation's economy, was pursued with great enthusiasm and at considerable expense."[12] American history is ripe with examples of extensive state governmental intervention in their economies.

The American states had borrowed heavily from English mercantilist practices in the seventeenth and eighteenth centuries. Mercantilism, a much older economic tradition than laissez faire, stressed the importance of governmental intervention. One of the major problems confronting the early American colonies was a shortage of capital resources. Colonial governments attempted to mitigate this problem by creating incentives and opportunities to stimulate needed forms of economic activity. By providing legal frameworks for private enterprise they fostered agriculture, industry, and commerce. Fiscal controls such as import or export duties and tax exemptions were used to stimulate targeted endeavors such as iron and nail making, hemp growing, woolen mills, and sailcloth making. Monopolies were granted as well as direct aid in the form of land grants, loans to stimulate creation of cotton manufacturing, iron works and the like, and bounties that functioned much like contemporary subsidies.[13]

These governments also collected and disseminated useful information to promote certain industries. Finally, states established joint public-private ventures when particular services were essential or private capital was lacking.[14]

The new American economy suffered a severe recession in the wake of the revolution but then began a period of accelerated economic growth. This growth was stimulated largely by the opening of interior markets through the development of a transportation network that greatly increased the flow of trade and the establishment of manufacturing. Road building and maintenance continued to be a state and local function, states providing direct aid to meet the large capital requirements of transportation projects. The most famous and successful of these ventures was the Erie Canal, constructed by the state of New York for $7 million. L. Ray Gunn provides an enlightening account of the political processes that led to the creation of the Erie Canal in *The Decline of Political Authority* (1988). New York State intervened to construct the Erie Canal with public funds after several private ventures had failed. The state invoked the "public interest" as justification for intervention in the economy and brought about dramatic economic change that otherwise would not have occurred. The Erie Canal was an enormous economic success which opened marginally accessible rural areas to markets, and touched off explosive economic growth by reducing farm to market transportation costs. The success of this canal sparked similar ventures by many other states, including Ohio, Indiana, Illinois, Virginia, and South Carolina. Pennsylvania built almost 700 miles of canals with $18 million of public funds. In his classic study of that state, Louis Hartz observed that

> in the face of the evidence it would be hard to contend that the objectives of economic policy cherished by the state from the time of the Revolution to the Civil War were either limited or unimportant. They ramified into virtually every phase of business activity, were the consistent preoccupations of politicians and entrepreneurs, and evoked interest struggles of the first magnitude. *Government assumed the job of shaping decisively the contours of economic life.* [emphasis added][15]

Clearly, states were intervening early in a multitude of economic activities to stimulate production and creation of industries to promote economic development. State intervention and financing of canals and other forms of transportation contributed significantly to early economic growth. States with higher capacity for intervention, such as New York, outraced the economic performance of other states.

Through the first third of the nineteenth century, state government intervention was widespread. However, state activity was to subside when a fiscal crisis, largely the result of substantial government expenditure without fiscal coordination, emerged. Public ire focused on government spending practices. Public finance decisions were decentralized and influenced by diverse and fragmentary interests in the state. In the wake of the Panic of 1837, state government was viewed with suspicion. In this era, a "revulsion against internal improvements" emerged among the states.[16] State constitutions began to prohibit state loans to private companies. New York's new constitution restrained the state's government. In the wake of fiscal crisis and allegations of corruption New Yorkers had a choice between continuing with activist government or reducing the powers of their government and its role in their economy. As Gunn notes, "Failure in the public mind, became synonymous with corruption; lack of power to govern was translated into abuse of power."[17] The government's role in the economy contracted. Public works construction was curtailed in 1842. In other states, too, legislative excesses and fiscal crises led to reform and restriction of state economic intervention by the middle of the nineteenth century.

THE LATE NINETEENTH CENTURY

National Political Economic Conditions. In general, the role of the federal government did not expand enormously in the immediate aftermath of the Civil War. However, the Civil War stimulated industrial development through direct government demand and capital reserves created by greenbacks and war profits. In this period corporate endeavor flourished and laissez faire became the economic doctrine of the era.

Federal intervention in the economy occurred in relatively subtle ways. Industrialization and a higher protective tariff brought increased revenues to the federal government during and immediately following the Civil War. These surplus revenues allowed the federal government to pay off the Civil War debt expeditiously. Due at least in part to its increased spending in 1865, the House of Representatives created the Appropriations Committee to relieve the overburdened Ways and Means Committee. This dual committee system for taxing and spending would remain until 1885, when members voted 227 to 70 to abolish the Appropriations Committee in favor of specialized appropriations committees to consider spending items.

Dissatisfaction with the Appropriations Committee in 1885, according to Richard Fenno, "lay primarily in the image of an excessively independent Appropriations Committee, with an undercurrent of criticism of an excessive economy-mindedness."[18] The desire of House members voting to abolish the Appropriations Committee was to tax and spend more. In succeeding years, spending measures concerning rivers and harbors, military procurement, the post office, and Indian affairs were given to substantive legislative committees. The result was the emergence of what are today called "iron triangles" or "unholy alliances": mutually beneficial relationships between bureaus, interests affected by bureaus, and congressional committees affected by bureau activities. In the 1890s roughly fifteen House committees and five Senate committees became involved in spending and logrolling became rampant. Government spending increased and public projects became more widespread. The era has been described by one historian as "the era of national subsidy." In this new era exalting laissez faire, government was not to directly construct or manage internal improvement projects, but to support such projects through subsidy with very little interference.[19]

The United States Supreme Court came to be a more important agent of this new economic order than Congress. Stephen Skowronek documents the enlarged role and capacity of federal courts in this period in *Building a New American State* (1982). From the 1870s through the 1890s, the Supreme Court molded new powers for itself by articulating principles of nationalism, substantive due process, and constitutional laissez faire wherein the court sharpened the boundaries between the public and private spheres. In 1890 a system of federal appellate courts was created by Congress that further increased the reach of the federal judiciary. Efforts to intervene or regulate business by states were often struck down by the federal judiciary in this era.[20]

As will be noted below, states had sought to regulate corporate endeavor during this era. In deciding what have become known as the Granger cases the U.S. Supreme Court had upheld the right of the states to regulate private property when that private property was affected with a public interest. The Court articulated three main principles for state intervention. First, as noted, states could regulate all businesses when they were affected with a public interest. Second, the Court held that it was the right of a state legislature to determine what is fair and reasonable. Third, it was the right of the states to act in areas of concurrent authority where Congress had failed to act.[21]

The regulatory role of states was very short-lived. A decade after the Granger cases the Supreme Court had a much more conservative composition. In the Wabash Case in 1886 the Court declared that an Illinois statute infringed on the exclusive power of Congress over interstate commerce.[22] In *Chicago, Milwaukee and Saint Paul Railroad Co. v. Minnesota* in 1890 the Supreme Court declared rate regulation by a state legislative commission to be constitutionally invalid.[23] Between

1877 and 1886 the Supreme Court set aside fourteen state laws directed at commerce. By the 1890s the Supreme Court had greatly curtailed the regulatory power of the states.

By reversing their position from the Granger cases, the Supreme Court placed the burden of regulation on the national government. In 1887, the Interstate Commerce Act was passed by Congress. The act established the Interstate Commerce Commission, composed of five members appointed by the President with the advice and consent of the Senate. Members served staggered terms at the pleasure of the President with a maximum of six years. The commission was largely ineffective at providing meaningful regulation. Vague and indefinite language left it to courts to interpret the act's meaning and in early cases the courts nullified the act. The Supreme Court reduced the ICC to little more than a statistics gathering agency, and for all practical purposes the commission had effected no change in the established mode of business conditions in this country.[24]

In this era, the national government created an environment that was very fruitful for corporate endeavor. The protective tariff created a prosperous economic context for corporate development. The Supreme Court's laissez-faire doctrines restricted the states from intervening in their own economies while national regulation was largely ineffectual. Hence, while the national government came to dominate the American political economy in this period, it was really an era dominated by the emergent power and wealth of corporations. As noted by one historian, the courts favored capitalists over trade unions, creditors over debtors, and railroads over farmers and consumers.[25]

State Economic Intervention. Like the American economy generally, American state politics came to be heavily influenced by corporations in this era. Ironically, before the Civil War state governments had intervened to encourage incorporation to stimulate economic development. The idea behind general incorporation was to relinquish governmental controls in favor of the laws of the marketplace. Railroad incorporation acts of the 1850s were quite successful in promoting railroad construction and came to dominate politics and economics in the post–Civil War era. As noted by Skowronek, the American railroad industry came to be something of a Frankenstein's monster by the end of the nineteenth century: "It had overpowered its sponsors at the state level, and finding no higher authority capable of providing supervision, it had become unruly and disruptive."[26] Rail mileage had doubled in America between 1870 and 1876. Proliferation of new roads could lead to the underutilization of existing carrying capacity and contribute to destructive forms of competition. The long-term interest of the railroads lay in mutual cooperation to divide traffic, fix rates, and ensure a stable and predictable environment. Railroads had corrupted many state governments, preventing just taxation of their property and avoiding regulation. Bryce observed that "War is the natural state of an American railway toward all other authorities."[27] Rate fixing, discrimination, and unfair practices had created hardships for the residents in many states, particularly those in the Farmbelt.

The economic panic of 1873 stimulated corrective action in several states. The Granger campaign for railroad regulation had its greatest impact in the upper Mississippi Valley, where laws were aimed at securing lower rates, preventing rate discrimination, and insuring intense railroad competition. In California, Kansas, and Missouri further state aid to railroads was denied. Some states sought to recover land grants, others prohibited specific abuses such as rebates and passes, and others directly regulated rates and services.

One of the best examples of this type of intervention is found in Illinois. The Illinois constitution of 1870 directed the state legislature to pass laws to correct railroad abuses. Pursuant to this charter the state's legislature outlawed discrimination, established a maximum rate, and created a Railroad and Commerce Commission in 1873. These reforms influenced the passage of similar laws in Iowa, Minnesota, and Wisconsin in 1874. The Railroad and Commerce Commission later served as a model for the Interstate Commerce Commission. Within a few years the railroads of the Midwest were regulated by an extensive array of restrictive state legislation. As noted above, the United States Supreme Court upheld initially the validity of these state regulations in the Granger cases. By the 1890s, however, a conservative United States Supreme Court had greatly constricted the opportunities for states to regulate commerce within their boundaries.

THE TWENTIETH CENTURY

National Political Economic Conditions. By the end of the nineteenth century, many had come to question the wisdom of laissez faire, at least as it had come to be practiced. This doctrine, once heralded as a guarantee of equal opportunity, was now a mechanism of exploitation and inequality. Corporate capitalism, largely unfettered by government, had organized oligopolistically, engaged in trade practices that restricted competition, and concentrated wealth in enormous amounts among an increasingly smaller handful of industrialists. As this corporate power grew, and as state and local authority had proven ineffectual in curbing its excesses, the federal government finally intervened.

Under Theodore Roosevelt the national government expanded its role in the economic realm.[28] He became the first president to intervene in the economy in the midst of a national depression in 1907 during a banking panic, and he also promoted a greater regulatory role by the national government as well. Woodrow Wilson would also see the importance of the national government in maintaining fair competition.[29] After this burst of national-level intervention, however, the nation returned briefly to its myth of laissez faire. Presidents from Harding to Hoover expressed in varying degrees their commitments to free-market economics. The markets, however, would fail in 1929 as America experienced the worst depression in its history.

Franklin Roosevelt, elected in the depths of the depression in 1932, saw intervention in the economy by the national government as essential to restoring employment and income. To this end, he initiated a multitude of programs under the New Deal to modify the economy, stabilize prices, and manage social problems. Never a coherent set of policies, the New Deal was instead an array of ad hoc policies to combat immediate economic crises. The expenditures of the federal government in this era give an indication of the growth of federal intervention. In 1929, the federal government spent $3.3 billion but by 1939, it was spending $8.9 billion, a 270 percent increase; federal expenditure as a percentage of GNP went from 3.2 percent in 1929 to 9.7 percent in 1939.[30]

The New Deal ushered in a new era in American political economy. As noted by Carolyn Webber and Aaron Wildavsky: "The enduring legacy of the New Deal was acceptance by the American public of the doctrine that the federal government has ultimate responsibility for the economy. . . . There might be arguments about how large governments should grow, but the era of small governments was over."[31]

State Economic Intervention. In the opening decades of the twentieth century, many American states were centers of innovation, passing laws on workers' compensation, unemployment insurance, and public assistance. In many ways, the policies of the New Deal found their inspiration in policies first adopted in the states to regulate large corporations and establish minimum labor standards. Yet, the American states were ill-suited to cope effectively with the ravages of the Great Depression, an economic catastrophe with national and international origins. As noted above, the federal government expanded its activities dramatically during this economic catastrophe and came to be unquestionably the preeminent force in American politics. In this era of domination by the national government, state governments "were the fiscal stepchildren of the federal system."[32]

It is this period, characterized by a dominant federal role, that is most familiar to students of state political economy. State-level efforts to stimulate economic performance were not completely absent but had a very distinctive character. Most of these efforts were motivated by a desire by less developed states to attract mobile capital. James C. Cobb describes the efforts of southern states to attract industry such as Mississippi's Balance Agriculture with Industry program to lure northern industry by offering tax incentives and capitalizing on low labor costs. These programs should be viewed with caution, however, for their main goal was less the "public interest" than to maintain the established social order in the South. Cobb argues that these efforts promoted continuity as much as change. They left untouched the region's traditions of minimal government and did nothing to challenge upper-class white domination of southern society. Instead these efforts assured investors of a docile workforce, low taxes, and cooperative government.[33]

According to another economic historian, the transformation of the southern economy in the post–World War II era was less the result of their efforts to lure industry, and more the consequence of federal policy. Gavin Wright contends in *Old South, New South* (1986) that the closed political processes of the South produced policies that did not try to expand opportunities for all its citizens. Instead, federal pressures resulting from minimum wage and civil rights legislation worked to allocate greater income to the economically displaced in the region. In the end, the national economy absorbed the South and the region has continued to diversify as outsiders have moved in to exploit growing markets that resulted from this absorption.

Even when the industrial recruitment efforts of southern states are considered, it is safe to say that for much of the post–World War II period, the United States economy has been dominated by federal-level activities. The unfortunate consequence of this is that it has led many to overlook the traditional role of the states in shaping their economies. As one recent observer notes, state intervention "has been a routine state function since the American Revolution, ignored by scholars because the ideology of laissez faire denied its existence. It is safe to say that government policies, as much as entrepreneurial activities are responsible for the shape of American economic growth."[34] Viewed in this light, it is entirely likely that recent changes in the American political economy in the last decade are not a dramatic departure from past practice but instead represent a return to a strong

American political-economic tradition. The states may be reassuming their role in managing their economies.

Empirically, subtle hints have suggested that the role of the states in their economies has been increasing. Findings of studies of state-level political economy covering data from the 1940s to 1960s suggest little support for the hypothesis that state-level activity had any effect on state economic performance. For example, in a study of the 1949–59 period, Campbell detected no relationship between state taxes and growth.[35] Similarly, in a time series analysis of the 1950–60 period, Stryck found that while state taxes could harm growth, expenditure levels had no discernable effect on growth.[36] Complementing these studies, Browne concluded that investment per capita was not noticeably influenced by state policy in a study of the 1960–76 period.[37] Taken together, these early studies all point to essentially the same conclusion: state policies had little or no impact on state economic growth.

Studies conducted with more recent data suggest a different conclusion. In their influential study of the 1967–77 period, Plaut and Pluta's evidence showed that state business climate, tax levels, and expenditures are related to employment and capital stock growth.[38] In an examination of the 1970–80 period, Vedder reported evidence that state tax levels hurt economic growth,[39] and McHone that state economic incentives had a weak effect in the 1970–79 period.[40] Schmenner found evidence in the 1970–79 period that relocation decisions of firms were responsive to the educational, cultural and recreational amenities available in states,[41] and similarly, in a study of the 1979–82 period Bartik showed that while taxes may hurt, improved public services may help attract firms.[42] The dominant finding from these more recent studies is that state policies are economically consequential.

Erik Herzik's evidence points to the increasing salience of economic issues in the American states. He examined eighteen categories of topics mentioned by governors in their state of the state messages from the 1970s to the 1980s. In 1970 and 1973 governors in his study did not mention economic development. By 1988, only education was being mentioned more frequently than economic development. Thad Beyle has noted that economic development, once a cyclical concern, has now become almost a perennial issue.[43] At the state level the politics of economic development have also undergone important changes. Heightened efforts at economic development policymaking have emerged as states assume a larger role in research, development, and investment. One observer has described this as a rise of the entrepreneurial state.[44] Another argues that "states have become lead-

ers in confronting the global challenge to American competitiveness."[45]

A new and growing literature on the American states has focused
on these emerging efforts by state governments to stimulate their
economies and promote economic development. Some of these studies provide little more than journalistic accounts of state actors and
events, or inventory recent changes that have taken place.[46] Several
accounts provide compelling arguments that fundamental changes
have taken place within the states in the last two decades. Most
notably, Peter Eisinger argues that "subnational economic development policy has undergone a recent shift from an almost exclusive
reliance on supply-side location incentives to stimulate investment to
an approach that increasingly emphasizes demand factors in the market as a guide to the design or invention of policy."[47] He believes this
change represents a restructuring of longstanding relations between
the public and private sectors in the states.

R. Scott Fosler has compiled a series of essays that complements
the basic thrust of Eisinger's argument.[48] Written by both academicians
and policymakers, the accounts in Fosler's volume all underscore the
increasing importance of state governments in shaping state economic
performance. Government action is not construed in wholly negative
terms. Political institutions may play a positive role in economic development by working to identify economic problems and then serving to formulate and implement policies to rectify those problems. In
its conventional role, the state passively accepted prevailing economic
forces under the assumption that national economic growth was more
or less inevitable. In its new role, "the state employs an active strategy
to improve its economic competitiveness by confronting and taking
advantage of prevailing economic forces."[49] Fosler underscores the
importance of the capacity of political institutions for adjusting to new
and changing economic forces.

These studies have described in rich detail the kinds of economic
development policies that have emerged in many states.[50] They not
only argue that the states have become more active, but that their
activism is qualitatively different in this period from what they have
undertaken in the past. To be sure, certain important aspects of economic development have remained largely constant: the use of public-
private partnerships and decentralization in the design and implementation of policies; the focus on providing support for capital rather
than labor; the pragmatic rather than ideological criteria used to make
decisions and evaluate policies; and the minimal degree of planning
undertaken (although more than in the past). Yet, what has captured
the attention of most observers are the differences between economic

development policies of the past and those that have appeared recently. In particular, the latter reflect a markedly different style of intervention in the market, new policy goals, and modifications in the way policy instruments and resources are deployed.

Instead of passively accepting prevailing economic forces and federal economic policy as givens in their environment, state governments have sought to anticipate economic change and take advantage of it in ways that improve competitiveness. Eisinger encapsulates this new style of intervention in the phrase "the entrepreneurial state." Here the state, in partnership with private business, becomes an active player in the market rather than simply a residual reactor to the decisions made by others. Whether underwriting and encouraging new product development, basic and applied high-tech research, or the adoption of new production processes in mature industries, the entrepreneurial state acts as "a risk-taker and path-finder to new markets."[51] Much like the classic individual entrepreneur, the state seeks "to exploit opportunities that are generally not apparent to other decision-makers."[52]

Ultimately, of course, the goals of current economic development policies are the same as they have always been: a stable and growing economy, and consequently, higher levels of income and employment. At another level, however, the goals have changed and expanded dramatically. Until the 1970s the goal of economic development was the attraction of businesses from other states to replace lost employment and, perhaps, the retention of existing industries. These purposes have been superseded by a focus on the creation of new industries and markets and the expansion of existing ones.[53]

With these goals have come some new policy instruments, but more often existing instruments and resources have been deployed using new strategies that focus on the demand-side rather than the supply-side. The older supply-side approach sought to attract industries by providing incentives that lowered production-factor (capital, land, and labor) costs. They included, for instance, loans and loan guarantees to help finance investment, lower tax rates, tax exemptions, abatements, and incentives, right-to-work laws, job training, regulatory reform, and other programs to improve a state's "business climate" ranking.[54]

The inadequacy of the supply-side approach has led states to turn to the demand-side. The latter are justified on the grounds that they permit earlier and more decisive intervention in private investment decisions, help to avoid head-to-head competition in providing location inducements, and promise to promote real capital formation rather than simply relocate existing industries. Where the supply-side inducements focused on stimulating capital relocation or capital retention, the demand-side focuses on discovering, developing, expanding, and creating new markets for indigenous industries. Where, in the former case, government supported low-risk undertakings and did not discriminate between industries and firms by targeting assistance, in the latter government has become involved in high-risk enterprises and offers assistance selectively according to strategic criteria. In the supply-side approach government followed and supported private sector decisions about where to invest, what businesses would be profitable, and what products would sell; in the demand-side approach it helps identify new investment opportunities that private firms may have overlooked or been reluctant to pursue.

While new interpretations of state political economy point to the importance of state governments, the consequences of this state economic activity are not clear. None of these new accounts argues strongly that states are making a large difference in their economic performance. Eisinger is probably the most optimistic but he is only willing to say that these new demand-side initiatives "probably work."[55] Fosler is much more pessimistic. He notes that with a few exceptions "there is little evidence that the surge in state economic activism over the past decade or so has had a significant effect on stimulating the economic recovery and growth exhibited by the states following the recession of the 1980s."[56]

It appears that the states have come full circle. Economic activism is alive and well in many states. This activism is not new but is a return to a role that was dominant early in the nation's history, when the role of the federal government was much smaller and the global economy was very challenging for the new nation. Few states could labor under the assumption that national economic growth is inevitable. Nor could their growth be taken for granted. There are many parallels with the setting of the contemporary states. After 200 years of experience, however, we do not know the answer to a very fundamental question: Does state economic intervention help, hurt, or have any effect at all?

The Economies of States within the Nation

At this point some of the main lessons from American political economic history can be recited. First, there have been several political economies over the course of American history. Second, the states have approached economic matters differently over time, depending on the activities of the national government. Early on the states were economic activists. Later, the states attempted to regulate corporations and control some of the economic hardships created by corporate capitalism. In each instance, the activities (or lack thereof) by the national government created the impetus for state level activities. Examining much of the post–World War II context, the activities of the national government virtually suffocated state-level efforts. The enormous fiscal resources of the federal government, with its progressive income tax and ability to deficit spend, dwarfed the states, typically forced by their constitutions to balance their budgets, which are tied to the vicissitudes of revenues based on sales taxes and user fees. In this era, the policies of the federal government had the effect of "nationalizing" the U.S. economy, with economic development being distributed to many formerly less developed states.

State political economy becomes more understandable when the dynamic historical context of the states is incorporated in our thinking. To unravel the mystery of political economy we need to consider two dimensions of state economic development: *national context* and *state capacity*. *National context* refers to the national political and economic setting in which states exist. This context is not static but has been shaped by cycles, with primary governmental responsibilities oscillating between federal and state levels over time. The nation's economy, too, may be considered to have a national and state component. In national economic eras all states may experience growth, while in other eras growth may be distributed sectorally, with some states outpacing others.

State capacity refers to the governmental and political resources available within a state to manage or modify its economy. States vary dramatically in the power and professionalism in their political institutions, in the amounts they tax and spend, and in the degree to which they intervene in their economies. Some states score highly on almost all of these attributes and others score very low. State government capacity, furthermore, varies significantly between the regions, with southern and southwestern states scoring quite low in all categories, and northern and midwestern states scoring highly.

State capacity has a cost in terms of taxation to support administration, infrastructure, and state intervention in the economy. States with greater capacity would be at a comparative disadvantage when growth was coming to the nation in general. In such a context, those states with less capacity would have a comparative cost advantage to those financing much larger public sectors. In these eras, neoconservative laissez-faire interpretations of states and their economies would seem to fit best: states taxing, spending, and intervening least would be growing most.

TABLE 2. State Capacity and National Context

		State Capacity	
		High	Low
National Economic Context	Nationally Dominant	Decline	Dependent Growth
	State Dominant	Self-Sufficient Growth	Decline

The capacity of states may play a much different role in a more challenging economic context. In a national context, where growth could not be taken for granted, state effort to sustain growth could be instrumental for economic progress. In these eras the capacity of state government to invest, construct and maintain infrastructure, educate its citizenry, and otherwise direct more substantial public resources in economic intervention could be critical for stimulating state economic performance.

The expected influence of context and capacity leads to hypotheses about the role of the states in shaping their economic performance. These hypotheses are highlighted in Table 2. Within this framework, the economic impact of the state is contingent on the context in which states exist. An effective strategy in one setting could be horribly disadvantageous in another, as will be seen in the four state case studies. The framework leads us to consider how the effects of state-level political capacity, independent of the nation's economy, may affect state economic performance. In addition, since the interplay of national influences on state economic performance is not static, we must also consider how this context might change over time, particularly over the last two decades.

To evaluate the changing state-national economic nexus suggested above, two issues are explored in the systematic evaluation of the economic contexts of states presented in chapter 5. First, how dependent are state economies on the performance of the national economy? Second, has this pattern of dependence changed? Results of this analysis will reveal that a fundamental change in state political economy was initiated during the Reagan Administration. In this new political economy, states have come to display greater economic diversity, at least suggesting that state-level capacity may be playing a greater role.

The hypothesis that state capacity is playing a greater role in a new and more challenging economic environment is tested in chapter 6. At the state level, state economies are reasoned to be influenced by their capacity: the capacity of their political institutions, their economic policymaking, their taxing and spending policies, and the nature of party control. The economic consequences of these attributes are examined in a model that controls for important alternative explanations for state economic performance as well. The model of state political economy is applied prior to 1982 and after 1982 to assess the changing role the states have come to play in the wake of changes initiated early in the Reagan Administration. The implications of the analysis and reflections on political economy in the American states will be presented in the concluding chapter.

It is the premise of this study that state political economy remains a mystery only if the major features of the enigma are ignored. A realistic portrait of state political economy begins with a background dominated by national economic conditions. When the shifting tide of national economic conditions and policies are taken into consideration, a more realistic appraisal of state-level effects can be offered. Understanding this interplay can reveal why diametrically opposed prescriptions can be offered by economic theorists and policymakers, and why these prescriptions appear variously to succeed and fail in different parts of the country at different times.

CHAPTER 3

The Political Economy of Dependence in Arizona and Texas

Anything that purports to be business is not . . . critically examined. State government exists for the purpose of facilitating business deals.
Former Arizona Governor Bruce Babbitt

"Good business climate" has been as sacred as the Alamo in Texas.
New York Times

The American states provide both an interesting and perplexing environment in which to explore the interplay of government and economics. The states contain a wide variety of governmental and policy differences which provide useful comparisons and allow for systematic evaluation of the consequences of government and policy on economies over time. They are perplexing, however, because they have exhibited vastly differing political-economic strategies which, at various times, have appeared both to work and to fail. Within the multiple and perplexing array of state economic activity, some states stand out.

In the 1960s and 1970s, the words Sunbelt and boom became almost synonymous. Arizona and Texas were the embodiment of the Sunbelt boom and, just as these states became synonymous with growth, their approach to politics and economics was viewed as responsible for their explosive growth. Based on their experience it appeared that the key ingredients for stimulating economic growth were open shops, low public expenditures, narrowly circumscribed political institutions, and probusiness orientations. The once stagnant economies of southern states and the underdeveloped economies of many western states flourished in the postwar era generally and in the seventies particularly. These states, of which Arizona and Texas are prime examples, outraced the economic growth of most other states and their growth was particularly dramatic when compared to eastern and midwestern states, where the reach of government in the economy was significantly longer, public programs were more expansive, and political institutions were more formidable. The comparisons were striking and the conclusions strong: growth came to those who created conditions favorable to business, decline came to those with expansive government sectors.

This interpretation also fits well with the popular but historically unsupported belief that at the core of American prosperity is a laissez-faire approach to the marketplace. What this account fails to consider is that the growth of these states (and others like them) may have resulted more from outside forces, rather than from the business climates they nurtured. The sensitivity of these economies to external factors became particularly apparent in the middle to late 1980s when these states suffered severe economic setbacks despite the probusiness environments they had labored long and hard to create. National and international forces had stemmed the tide of their growth, calling into question the viability of their approach to economic development. The economic setbacks experienced by Arizona and Texas, despite their aggressive efforts to create favorable business conditions, suggests that their growth and decline was outside their control. Thus, the explosive growth in the post–World War II era may have come *despite* their governments and public policies, not because of them. Before we can assign blame or award accolades to state governments and their economic development strategies, we must first consider the economic contexts in which they exist, and how much of their economies are legitimately within their control.

Arizona

POLITICAL AND ECONOMIC TRADITIONS

Early History. From its very beginnings Arizona was founded on a fundamental incongruity between belief and reality. Arizona is unique among states in that most of its earliest settlers came from the West instead of the East. Many of the territory's early residents moved there from California, seeking opportunities in the unfettered territory of Arizona. The territorial ethos of individualism pervades the state to this day, coloring many discussions of government and politics. Politicians and business leaders extol the virtues of economic independence and condemn governmental encroachment. Yet this ethos of rugged individualism and self-reliance fails to consider a fundamental feature of the Arizona economy. it has been nurtured by the federal government and by abundant natural resources.

Even in its territorial beginnings, Arizona's economic development was highly dependent on its natural resources and on the policies of the federal government. Growth that results because of mineral wealth or federal largesse, however, should be distinguished from growth that occurs because of the conditions created by the state. Thus, in examining the rhetoric of free-market individualism in this state, it is worth remembering that this rhetoric is delivered from a stage that was built to a large degree on the value of the state's mineral wealth and by infusions of federal capital.

For most its early history Arizona relied on the "Three C's" of cotton, cattle, and copper. Contrary to popular myth, early settlers did not live in isolation on the frontier but instead were clustered in towns: mining, irrigation, and Indian attacks worked to concentrate populations. Almost from the territory's inception, its residents were highly dependent on the U.S. military for protection from Apache tribes, which determined largely where the settlers could reside. The settlers benefited further by providing supplies to the military. Phoenix, the state's largest population center, was founded in 1867 as a hay camp for the cavalry at Fort McDowell. In addition, many farmers prospered by selling their products to the military in camps north of Phoenix. Hence, from the very beginning the economy of Arizona was bolstered by and dependent on the defense policies of the U.S. government, rather than individualistic and independent as it is often portrayed.

The state's reliance on its mineral resources also influenced the organization and character of industry in the state. Large mining operations gave rise to early labor disputes and bloody conflicts with management. In the 1880s mining companies employed many Mexican Americans in unsafe working conditions and for wages that were substantially less than white workers received. An early mutual aid society was formed that eventually became the Western Federation of Miners. This union challenged the enormous power of the mining companies and the mining companies responded. In 1871, vigilantes in the Bisbee Workman's Loyalty League and Citizen's Protective League rounded up 2,000 local workers. They released those willing to condemn the union while any that would not recant union philosophy were deemed undesirable. The vigilantes placed almost 1,200 on boxcars and shipped them out of the state. This incident severely weakened labor unions in the state. Arizona would become a right-to-work state in 1946 when voters approved the addition of Article 25 to the state's constitution. Today the proportion of unionized workers in the state is third lowest in the nation.

From statehood in 1912 until the 1950s the Democratic party dominated politics in Arizona. The party controlled the state legislature until the 1960s. As noted in one account of the state's politics, the Democratic party of Arizona was controlled by copper, cattle, cotton, and the utilities and, apart from a brief wave of populism during the 1910 state constitutional convention, the party was very conservative, in many ways similar to southern Democrats.[1]

The Democratic party was divided between a labor-progressive wing, which drew its support from mining towns, and a conservative faction dominated by interests from cotton, cattle, and copper. The conservative faction dominated the legislature while the progressive-labor faction controlled the governorship. Arizona's early residents came from the South via California. The pre-eminent concern of the dominant "Pinto democrats" of this era was with getting more support from the federal government.

Despite Democratic dominance of state politics and the party's majority in voter registration, Arizona went with Republican presidential candidates in 1920, 1924, 1928, and 1952. The pulling power of the Republican presidential candidates pulled seven Republicans to state-wide office in 1920, and four additional statewide victories in 1952.[2]

Defense came to play a different but equally important role in Arizona's twentieth century economic development. During World War I, Goodyear Tire and Rubber contracted with the federal government to produce cotton for military tires and airplane fabric. The company constructed a major cotton processing facility and built the community of Litchfield Park to house company managers and workers. According to one account, Goodyear encouraged Arizona Senator Carl Hayden to lobby for an air force base and in 1941 Luke Air Force Base was built.[3] Expanded military operations during World War II and Arizona's proximity to Los Angeles and the Pacific Theater brought more defense dollars to the state and defense-related industries also continued to expand, setting the stage for Arizona's economic development after the war.

The Post–World War II Era. The aftermath of the Second World War ushered in a new era in Arizona's economic development. Owing to aggressive efforts by the state, Motorola relocated to Phoenix in this period, as did Greyhound (aided by a new Arizona law that gave tax breaks to companies moving their headquarters to the state). Pro-business interests succeeded in lowering taxes and actively recruited businesses to the state. This practice of luring employers with tax breaks and other incentive practices, called "buffalo hunting," originated earlier in the century in southern states. Some have questioned the long-term effects of this practice because often the incentives and other costs to the state from a business relocating in this manner (such as increased demands for schools and transportation) outweigh the additional revenue these businesses bring to the state. In this era, however, Arizona flourished as new businesses came to the state and many new residents arrived, attracted by low-cost real estate and recreational amenities in a state made more palatable by the increasing availability of air conditioning.

As Arizona grew it changed politically. Democratic dominance diminished as mining declined in importance and this Democratic constituency found itself diluted by new residents lured to the state by high-technology jobs and abundant recreational resources. By the 1960s the Republican party assumed a dominant position throughout the state. Where the party had won only 7 percent of the major offices from 1911 to 1950, it captured 48 percent of these offices from 1952 through 1982.[4] With redistricting in 1966 the Republicans went from 2 of 28 to 16 of 30 seats in the state Senate, and from 16 of 30 to 33 of 60 seats in the state House. The Republican party also gained in voter registration, going from a 1 to 10 deficit in the wake of World War II to a virtual standoff with the Democrats in the early 1980s.[5]

Supplanting old-style Democratic politics that had focused on attracting federal defense installations and water projects were a probusiness conservatism and Republican domination of the state's politics. In this era, the state's economic development came increasingly to be viewed as the result of private business decisions. The modern transformation of the state has seen the three C's surpassed in importance by manufacturing, tourism, real estate, and service industries.[6]

In this period the state's business *was* business and the ensuing pattern of economic growth did little to challenge the viability of this approach. The most phenomenal growth in Arizona came in the 1970s. During this decade personal income increased almost 90 percent, over double the national average; employment increased at three times the national average; and population expanded at almost five times the nation's rate.[7]

Arizona's manufacturing base expanded rapidly as firms and industries relocated to the state. As the state boomed, its reliance on its traditional mainstays of agriculture and mining declined although through the 1970s these interests retained significant clout.[8] Real estate and other developers emerged as alternative, although often complementary, interests in the 1960s and modified the monolithic power structure to a limited degree. Arizona's rapid development and conservative, probusiness politics fueled the perception inside and outside the state that the road to economic prosperity was through unrestricted free enterprise. As David Osborne observes, however, without federal expenditures for military bases, defense plants and dams, the state would still be a rural backwater.[9] By the 1980s, government provided the most income and employment in the state.[10]

The politics of Arizona reflect the ethos of business and rugged individualism despite the enormous importance of government to the state's economy. In the early 1980s, for example, business comprised roughly 69 percent of interest group activity within the state. The second highest category of interest groups (the professions and health) comprised only 7 percent of the state's interest groups. Organized labor is notoriously weak in the state, owing largely to Arizona's "Right-to-Work" law. By the early 1980s organized labor constituted only 1 percent of the state's interest groups. Employment growth in high-tech industries has remained unorganized; farm workers have seldom succeeded in organizing; and booms and busts in the construction trades have hindered labor's cohesion there.[11]

Policymaking in Arizona in this era placed conservative legislators in concert with heavily represented business interests. There were few countervailing forces. Added to this, the legislature had little institutional capacity, ranking 43 out of 50 state legislatures in effectiveness in 1971.[12] Given the complexion of the organized interests, the ideological leanings of the politicians, and the ineffectiveness of the state's political institutions, it is not surprising that the state would extol the virtues of hands-off economic strategies.

In the postwar era, Arizona was under little pressure to stimulate its own economy. Reflective of the state's laissez-faire attitude, its economic development strategy amounted to little more than a favorable tax climate to attract industry.[13] The most pressing economic issue for Arizona during this boom era was dealing with too much growth. As small towns grew to sizable cities and cities sprang up where nothing had existed before, growth outraced the ability of political institutions to cope with it. The state's ethos of individualism and antigovernment sentiment contributed to a tradition of minimal commitment to important state-funded activities such as higher education. Oddly, the antigovernment posture that many viewed as instrumental to Arizona's phenomenal growth began to undermine that growth in the 1970s. Even while high-tech industries in Arizona boomed, they began having trouble recruiting engineers because of the underfinanced engineering program at Arizona State University.

A paradox between the state's underdeveloped public sector and its economic development ambitions soon became apparent. After a visit by its president, the MCC corporation announced that Arizona was not on its list of finalists as a location site. One of the reasons stated for this decision was that the state had not developed educational excellence in engineering and research.[14] High-tech industries, it appeared, needed more than a laissez-faire business environment: they needed a well-educated workforce and technological support.

A New Economic Era. The bloom on Arizona's approach to economic development began to wilt in the late 1980s. Growth slowed dramatically and the Arizona economy began to show signs of losing some of its seemingly unstoppable buoyancy. For the first time in decades, Arizona's unemployment rate went above the national average. In 1989 when national wage and salary nonagricultural employment grew at 3.1 percent, in Arizona it grew at only 1.3 percent, ranking it 41 out of the 50 states.

The construction and real estate industries were at the heart of the economic slowdown. These industries had burgeoned with the seemingly unstoppable influx of migrants to the states in the 1970s and early 1980s. With the economic recovery in the Frostbelt and the energetic California economy to the west, this migration slowed during the mid 1980s. Net migration to the state fell from a high of 90,000 in 1985 to 36,000 in 1988.[15] Residential housing permits fell by one-third. The vacancy rate hovered between 12 to 15 percent. By 1988, office vacancies in Phoenix were at 20 percent, apartment vacancies at 17 percent, and large numbers of homes sat vacant because owners were unable to sell or rent them.

The slump in construction had predictable repercussions on the real estate market. Prices on property that had risen during the boom years collapsed. Savings and loan institutions failed: six of the state's twelve thrifts were under government control or were insolvent in 1989. Developers and investors in the states suffered from massive cash flow problems and lenders' loan portfolios have been backed by land of increasingly dubious value. In 1988, Arizona had the fifth largest increase in filings among United States bankruptcy districts in 1988. While the diminished performance of the Phoenix economy drew the most attention, weaknesses also emerged in the economy of Tucson. In late 1988, vacancies in industrial buildings stood at 40.9 percent, offices at 25.4 percent, shopping malls at 14.2 percent, and apartments at 11.7 percent.[16]

While many focused on the severe downturn in Arizona real estate and the related crisis in the state's banking institutions, there were other problems that clouded the state's economic outlook. The much anticipated high-technology explosion never really materialized. Cuts in defense spending also threatened to slow growth in manufacturing jobs in Arizona. And while the conditions in the two major metropolitan areas were bad, outlying areas were worse. Rural Arizona had not experienced anything like the booms that had occurred in Phoenix and Tucson and conditions were magnified in traditionally poor areas as the state's economy declined.

Arizona's manufacturing sector could not offset the losses in real estate and construction. In 1988, IBM shut down its manufacturing operations and reduced its workforce there by 2,500. Hughes Aircraft laid off roughly 1,000 workers in the wake of budget trimming in Washington.[17] With one of the highest concentrations of high-tech employment in the country, the state was particularly hard hit by increasing global competition in high-technology industries, especially when the semiconductor industry began to move substantial production to Mexico in 1986.

According to some reporters, an ominous cloud had settled over Arizona, and especially Phoenix, by the late 1980s. Where once terms such as "The Phoenix Phenomenon" and "Boomtown USA" were used, a pervasive pessimism came to color many discussions of the Phoenix and the Arizona economy. A report in *Barron's* observed: "For all its pretensions to major city status, Phoenix remains a locale arrested in development between brash adolescence and adulthood." This article detected "unmistakable signs of a deep and protracted real estate bust."[18] While many Arizonans would challenge this account, the mere appearance was a clear sign that all was not well in this preeminent growth state. In the depths of their economic crisis, some were referring to Arizona's slump as "Texas II" or "Texas: The Sequel."[19]

It is interesting that, in a state that has long heralded the virtues of limited government and which attributed its economic success to a lack of government intervention, some have been quick to blame government for the economy's downturn. As reported in the *Arizona Republic*, "Many businessmen contend that elected officials, both on the state and local levels, have failed to produce effective long-run economic development plans . . . and have failed to make economic development a top priority, apparently choosing by inaction to let the economy develop haphazardly." The same story observed that "no one has come forward with the ability to build the coalitions necessary to solve problems and coalesce the state's fractious economic-development effort."[20] It is somewhat ironic, but perhaps not surprising, that the business community that would attribute Arizona's economic successes to a lack of government would be quick to blame its economic failures on a lack of political capacity.

By the beginning of the 1990s, Arizona faced new economic challenges as conditions continued to worsen. In 1991 job growth was at its lowest rate since 1982. Bankruptcy was up by 10 percent as a record 19,687 petitions were filed in the state.[21] The state's major employer, America West Airlines, filed for Chapter 11 protection in June. Circle K, another major Arizona business, announced plans to close or sell 1,600 of its stores, including 70 to 100 in Arizona. Defense-related firms laid off thousands of workers. The state's unemployment rate climbed from 5.7 percent in January to 7.3 percent in November. While there was growth in the service sector, some state economists believed those low-paying jobs would be a drain rather than an aid to the state's economy.[22]

In Arizona, as in many other states, the failure of savings and loan institutions plagued the economy. The problem was particularly salient in Arizona because Fife Symington, the state's newly elected governor, was a former official of a failed savings and loan institution. In December of his first year of office, the governor was sued and accused of causing the thrift to lose millions of dollars through gross negligence in the use of depositors' funds.[23] Symington had been elected on a platform calling for the state to go on a fiscal diet. His approval plunged and by January of 1992 only 20 percent of Arizonans thought he was doing a good job.[24] Only the scandal-racked administration of Evan Mecham—who hit 13 percent before being impeached—had received lower approval. In another poll, 39 percent of the state's registered voters believed Symington should resign.[25]

With yet another scandal-ridden governorship, Arizona found itself ill-prepared to take the lead and respond aggressively to its economic problems. The financial outlook in the state continued to worsen. In this context, Governor Symington proposed a $60 million tax cut to boost the state's flagging economy. In announcing the plan, Symington stated that "we cannot expect to revitalize our economy if we continue to saddle our people with additional tax burdens."[26]

It is not surprising that a Republican governor in Arizona would propose a tax cut in the midst of an economic crisis. Many in the state continue to believe that a favorable tax climate is the cornerstone of economic growth. This belief was summarized by Republican Senate Minority Leader Tom Patterson, who reasoned: "If we can just hold the line on taxes we will look good compared to other states."[27] Despite this prevailing outlook, there has been growing concern that this familiar strategy may not serve the state well in an increasingly complex and challenging national and international economy. Within both political parties, the importance of job training to give workers skills suitable for better paying jobs was acknowledged. Arizona remained one of only five states that had no state-supported job training program. A member of the Arizona Economic Council observed that "we have lost business in Arizona because of our inability to offer a state training program."[28] Despite this new awareness in the state, the possibilities for active state intervention appear bleak as diminished growth and tax cuts threaten the state's shrinking fiscal resources.

In the end, Arizona's politics have retained much of the color of its pioneer legacy and often chaos has prevailed in the state's governance with scandals plaguing both the executive and legislative branches. This weak and limited government has done little to support sustained and deliberate efforts to promote the economic well-being of the state. Instead, these politics fueled a tumultuous environment where programmatic effort could seldom emerge. Arizona continues to rely on two of its prime assets to stimulate its future growth. First, its climate remains an attractive attribute likely to lure population from the colder northern climates. Second, the state is an inexpensive place to live, particularly in comparison to neighboring California. The continuing reliance on these two factors underscores a central feature of Arizona's economic development scenario: the state is highly dependent on external forces to stimulate its economy. As long as conditions elsewhere stimulate migration to the state, and as long as it retains its relatively low cost of living compared to other states, Arizona can grow. When these forces are not operating, however, the state appears ill-suited for stimulating its own economic development.

While the global economy and changing technologies are bringing very new challenges to Arizona, many of the state's responses resemble the patterns evident in nineteenth century New York, where those benefiting most from economic growth had the financial and political resources to avoid shouldering their share of the burden for sustaining that growth. It would be hard to think of a better example of this than Arizona's government-bashing Republican governor, with a background in real estate, and mired in an S and L scandal, proposing a tax cut as a means to further prosperity. This posture, while sometimes successful in the past, may be sowing the seeds of its own failure as it becomes increasingly apparent that the capacity of the state to intervene may be essential for self-sustained growth.

Texas

POLITICAL ECONOMIC TRADITIONS

Early History. Texas has always prided itself on being different. Until this century Texas was enormous only in its geography and in its tall tales. In the past few decades, however, the state has become a major population center rivaling New York as the second most populous state. The Texas transformation has often placed incongruent images side by side: ranchers and oilmen alongside the aerospace industry, and enormously powerful interests alongside an antiquated and amateurish, part-time polity.

Historian Gavin Wright believes that the tradition of slavery had unobvious repercussions for the economy of the South. Slaves, according to Wright in *New South, Old South*, were very valuable assets that could be easily moved to take advantage of more fertile soil. Because wealth was primarily in slaves, planters had few ties to a local area. Without local commitments, they had little incentive to make long-term investments in other assets like land improvement, community development, or education. The result was an absence of towns, local political institutions, or schools in the antebellum South. With emancipation, land replaced slaves as the primary asset and planters needed a low-wage, unskilled workforce to exploit this asset. The lack of investment in schools and communities before the Civil War contributed to the unskilled character of the labor force after the war. Because of the abundance of unskilled labor, there were few incentives in the South to develop capital- or machine-intensive industries. Mechanization of cotton harvesting could have occurred much sooner but it was not until 1970s that most cotton became harvested mechanically.

Wright argues that the South had little incentive to invest in the education of its citizens because workers with increased skills could command higher wages. Its isolated labor market affected the choices of technology and the subsequent nature of political and economic development in the region. Political disorganization was characteristic of the South as blacks and whites of compatible economic interests were kept apart by the ever present issue of race. As V. O. Key aptly noted, this political disorganization worked to the advantage of the haves in southern society: political organization was necessary for promotion of policies to benefit the have-nots.[29] Comprehensive policies for things like education were absent, perpetuating the unskilled nature of the labor force.

When Texas entered the Union, all public land belonged to the state, not to the federal government. This accentuated the state's sense of independence. The lure of dirt-cheap ranches that attracted many to the state established a reverence for the rights of landowners to do whatever they wanted, without government interference. Perhaps the best example of this reverence is the lack of zoning ordinances in Houston.

Texas was the furthest extension of the slaveholding South and a very enthusiastic Confederate state. Many forces that shaped other southern states also shaped the history of Texas. The Texas economy, like the economy of the South generally, did poorly in the period following the Civil War. The long-run pattern of decline and recovery of the postbellum southern economy has drawn the attention of many historians and economists. In recent years economic research has emphasized the monopolistic character of the agricultural sector. This, combined with exploitative credit markets and emancipation without redistribution of land to freedmen created a situation in which workers were poor and plentiful and their wages kept extremely low. Economically speaking, the supply-side of the economy was well-fed but the demand-side was undernourished.[30]

The most significant economic event in the state's history occurred in East Texas in 1901 with the discovery of oil on Spindletop. Petroleum was discovered in Texas as early as 1866, and there were scattered efforts to discover and produce oil in the years that followed. In 1894, while drilling a water well for the city of Corsicana, a major oil deposit was discovered that subsequently became known as the Powell field. Spindletop, however, dwarfed all past discoveries. In 1900, oil production in Texas had been 836,000 barrels. In 1902, Spindletop alone produced 17.4 million barrels, accounting for 94 percent of the state's oil production. Spindletop broke the monopolistic hold on oil held by Rockefeller and the Standard Oil Company and permitted the entry of many new interests into the petroleum industry. It stimulated investment in oil exploration in the state. Over the next three decades there were major oil discoveries in the Texas Panhandle, East Texas, and the Gulf Coast. In 1930, the discovery of the East Texas Field was made on land previously abandoned by large petroleum companies. Oil created many instant millionaires. Oil and gas production also contributed to service and processing industries and stimulated a geological industry in Texas, which until that point had had almost no industry and very little commerce.

State and federal policies influenced the oil and gas industry heavily. At the federal level, large tax incentives, including the percentage depletion allowance and the provision for expensing of allowable drilling costs, stimulated the industry's growth. It was at the state level, however, that government's helping hand was most evident in the development of the oil and gas industry. In the 1930s, Texas petroleum accounted for roughly 40 percent of the nation's production. The state was particularly hard hit by the boom and bust nature of the petroleum industry. The major discovery in the East Texas Field released a glut of oil on an economy already ravaged by the Depression.

In 1932, the Texas Legislature authorized the Texas Railroad Commission to limit oil production to estimated market demand. Under this system, the three-member elected commission would estimate monthly demand for the state's oil and allocate the allowable production to the oil wells in the state. This process of "prorationing" went into effect in 1938 and continued through 1972, when the commission set the rate at 100 percent. In the 411 months in which prorationing was in effect, 100 percent production occurred in only 15.[31] The effect of the system was not only to control waste but to control prices. The significance of the Texas Railroad Commission was enormous in its early years but declined in importance over time as new sources of oil emerged.

The Post–World War II Era. The period following World War II witnessed the most dramatic transformation of the Texas economy. Added to oil and agriculture, defense expenditures came to play a major role in the modern development of the Texas economy. Installations like Fort Sam Houston, Kelly Field, and Corpus Christi Naval Air Station provided a stable source of wealth for the state. In World War II, Texas received more than its share of military installations and defense plants. In the Cold War era, Texas continued to obtain a large measure of defense spending. In 1965 Texas was second only to California in the amount of payroll disbursements for military and civilian salaries related to defense payrolls.[32] Large aircraft manufacturing facilities came to the state. Major producers such as General Dynamics and Chance Vaught Aircraft built large plants in Texas. The aerospace industry expanded rapidly with America's space race and stimulated the development of an electronics industry. Most notable among these industries was Texas Instruments, with most of its operations around Dallas. For many years, over a third of Texas Instruments' business was defense-related. In all, defense and related industries have served to complement the post–World War II growth experienced by Texas.

The confluence of industry migration and prosperity in the oil and gas industry provided Texas with extraordinary growth for much of the post–World War II era. The figures are impressive. For example, Texas ranked second only to Florida in the fast growing South in growth in manufacturing employment in the 1954–60 period; during the 1960–70 period it ranked first.[33] On most commonly accepted economic indicators, Texas was among the top handful of states in growth rates up through the 1970s.

An examination of the Texas economy would be incomplete if the momentous events of the early 1970s were not considered. In the wake of the Arab Oil Embargo of 1973 and the escalation of energy prices in the 1970s, the Texas economy flourished. The price of a barrel of crude oil increased fivefold during the 1970s.[34] As the 1980s began the state ranked among the top three states in growth in such categories as personal income, foreign trade, retail sales, manufacturing, bank deposits, and nonresidential construction. The economic fortunes of Texas have run almost opposite the nation's. Because of changing markets for oil, Texas escaped many economic perils of the 1970s and early 1980s. Instead, the economic downturns in the Frostbelt often stimulated migrations of workers to Texas, which was basking in the glow of its energy driven growth.

Like other southern states, Texas has had a tradition of closed politics. Voting participation has been very low and party organization factionalized or nonexistent. Institutionally weak governors have confronted amateurish legislatures and the result has been stalemate and few broad-based policies to promote the general welfare of the citizenry. The lack of political organization and weak political institutions have served as formidable impediments to broad-based public programs. The state's weak and fragmented political institutions could do little to challenge those who benefited from the status quo. The oil and land rich, for example, could block policies that would expand the public sector. The legislature was ill-suited to deal with hard times. As noted in one account, its incapacity is partly because it has been "insulated from difficult choices by ample oil and gas revenues and partly because of a long-prevailing belief that the best government governs least."[35]

The undemocratic political structures in the South insulated the region's lawmakers from pressures to regulate their economies or to provide for better education or infrastructure. In the post–World War II era, many footloose industries converged on the region to take advantage of its favorable tax climate. The problem, as one observer notes, was that "industrialists were less interested in schools or hospitals than in low taxes, and responsible political leadership was less important to them than freedom from regulation."[36] Thus, throughout the region, for much of the postwar boom, business leaders succeeded in convincing these often insulated politicians that it was economically beneficial to hold down taxes and maintain a "healthy" business climate to perpetuate growth.

Texas cultivated a very probusiness attitude and its economic development activity, as in other southern states, typically centered on efforts to attract "footloose" industries to the region by "buffalo hunting." Healthy incentive packages and special tax abatements, as well as the state's open-shop laws, minimal government intervention, and otherwise low taxes were heralded as the cornerstones of economic growth. Oil, gas, and infusions of defense dollars allowed Texans to take growth for granted and state government had to do little to develop revenues to finance public programs. Having oil, according to one observer, was like "growing up with an inheritance. The money's going to come whether you do right or not."[37] With only a few interruptions, Texas production of crude oil increased steadily for decades until it surpassed 1 billion barrels in the early 1950s.

There was no motive for the state's government to intervene actively in its economy to stimulate growth, raise revenues, or promote economic development policies. While ranking among the very top states on indices of economic growth, the state would concomitantly rank very low with respect to the level of development of its political institutions. For example, the Texas legislature remains biennial despite the trend toward annual sessions that has occurred in many states. The legislature ranks 37th in compensation for its members, paying only $7,200. The Texas governorship has typically ranked very near the bottom on indices of formal powers.[38] All too often, the weakness of the state's political institutions contrasted with its uninterrupted growth, reinforcing the belief that economies grow best when governments do the least.

The prosperity of the state seemed to shed favorable light on its probusiness, limited government choices if not on its public policies. The state still lacks income tax and typically ranks very low on tax effort indices. In terms of public policy, according to Sarah McCally Morehouse, "Texas fails to place well in any of the tests one might impose to measure output of state government in terms of serving its children, the poor, the old, and the sick."[39] While in 1988, the state ranked 33rd on spending for education as a percentage of per capita income, in 1982 it ranked last. In 1988 public education in Texas reached crisis proportions when a federal court ordered an overhaul of the state's system of financing public education.

A New Economic Era. The oil-driven growth came to a crashing halt in 1982. The price of crude oil fell from a high of $37 per barrel to a low of $10. The value of real estate in Houston dropped by as much as 30 percent, exceeding losses experienced by most major cities during the Great Depression.[40] The economic crash of the early eighties has shaken many deeply held beliefs and altered the oil-based political culture of Texas. When oil and gas flourished, tax revenues from these industries served as a major component of the state's fiscal base and allowed Texas to remain the last major industrialized state not to have an income tax. For example, in 1981 the oil and gas industry provided the state with 28 percent of all state taxes. In 1988, taxes from these industries accounted for only 9 percent of the state's revenues.

Without the revenues provided by the oil and gas industry, Texas has had to reevaluate its commitment to low taxes and to reconsider what promotes economic prosperity. Since it could no longer rely on its oil "inheritance," its government and policies have been under increasing pressure. As noted by Paul F. Roth, president of the Texas division of Southwestern Bell Telephone Company, a weak school system "wasn't such a crucial factor when oil and cotton fueled the Texas economy" but "today this weakness represents an economic time bomb."[41] Texas found itself in a very challenging economic environment in the 1980s and this environment has led many to question the value of its past approach to economic development.

Riding the Crests and Valleys of the Nation's Economy: Government and Growth in Two Dependent States

For many years Arizona and Texas pursued economic growth by staying poor. In order to keep wages down and bring in industry these states have been probusiness, an orientation normally translated into being antiunion and antigovernment. State investments in infrastructure and education have been quite low. In sum, these states were poised to attract prosperity from other parts of the country but did little to stimulate their prosperity. For many years, population migration, defense expenditures and, in the case of Texas, changing markets for oil, stimulated rapid growth in these economies.

States like Arizona and Texas have often dominated the thinking of those developing strategies for state economic development. Indeed, their impressive growth occurred against a backdrop of very minimal government activity. This minimal government, however, often reflected fragmented and closed polities whose operations were colorful at best and tragic at worst. Thus, we should be cautious in attributing too much responsibility for these states' growth to their political practices. It may just be that the growth that these states experienced occurred as the result of many larger external forces over which they had little or no control. Such growth, it may be added, could have occurred despite and not because of these states' political practices and policies.

Less economically and politically developed states like Arizona and Texas could absorb technology and production practices from the more developed industrial northeastern and midwestern regions. It is likely that Texas and Arizona were the fortunate beneficiaries of the U.S. economy in the post–World War II era. In a period of unprecedented national growth, technology and production became distributed throughout the U.S. as producers sought the competitive advantages offered in the South and West. These were exogenous, not endogenous, factors and they do not serve as a viable strategy for directing states in their efforts to sustain growth in the more competitive global economy.

As the national economy has slowed, and as industry and employment have increasingly shifted overseas, the endogenous political processes and policies of Arizona and Texas appear ill-suited to compete in the more complex global economy. This has been true for many southern and southwestern states. As one account notes, "In a global economy the low-wage jobs that once moved to Alabama or South Carolina are now more likely to move to Latin America or Asia."[42] Now many southern and southwestern states are struggling to overcome the consequences of their traditional political practices. The changing global economy has undermined low wage/low tax strategies, leaving these regions with comparatively unskilled and undereducated workforces. That which had served to recruit industry twenty years ago produced rates of illiteracy that are disadvantageous in a service-oriented, technologically driven economy.

While Texas and Arizona have suffered setbacks, we should be hesitant about declaring their economies dead. Given time, they will no doubt recover. If we want to understand the economic role of state politics, government, and policies, we should see these recoveries for what they are. A state may decline to the point of having "nowhere to go but up." Hence, in states with an overabundance of office space and housing, eventually market forces will drive the prices of each to the point where they will serve to lure migrants to the state, particularly as costs rise in other parts of the country. For example, during the 1980s many costs increased in the resurgent economies of the Northeast and Midwest. Labor shortages drove up the hourly wage. Workers at a fast food outlet near Boston received $7.50 an hour and this outlet still had trouble recruiting employees. While labor and real estate markets in these areas drive prices up, the probusiness climate, real estate bargains, and abundant (and usually nonunionized) labor of states like Texas and Arizona can again serve to stimulate migration of production to these states to exploit these substantial cost advantages. Note, however, that like much of their post–World War II prosperity, such recovery is contingent on forces over which these states have little control. They merely wait until external market forces place them in a position of comparative advantage. At present, Arizona development has stalled,[43] and Texas, while benefiting from rising oil prices in the wake of the Persian Gulf crisis, is much more cautious about its economic future.[44]

The economic experiences of Arizona and Texas highlight the importance of national economic conditions. They also lead to speculation as to what the economic performance of such lesser developed states would be without the boost provided by the nation's economy. How would these economies perform without stimulative external forces in more challenging economic times? The plight of Arizona and Texas in the late 1980s suggests that they were not on as firm an economic footing as some within the state wanted to believe. Politics and policy in these states seemed economically unimportant when external forces promoting growth diminished. It is under such circumstances that we may better understand the true effects of state government and policy on state economic performance.

CHAPTER 4

The Political Economy of Intervention in Michigan and New York

There is no "invisible hand" guiding us inevitably to a prosperous future.

From an economic study conducted by
the state of Michigan

The continued economic growth of the state is enhanced by the existence of comprehensive, coordinated and effective state economic development policies.

From legislation in the state of New York

The experiences of Arizona and Texas are instructive. These two re-source-based states, with relatively underdeveloped political processes and traditions of minimal government intervention, flourished during the 1960s and 1970s but came to be severely challenged as the national economy changed in the 1980s. This chapter examines two states with dramatically different development patterns. Michigan and New York were among the very first to experience the pains of the changing national economy. These states, with traditions of government intervention and substantial public sector capacity, moved early to mobilize public resources to stimulate economic growth. They are almost exact opposites to Arizona and Texas in terms of their postwar economic experiences and their economic development strategies, and illustrate a dramatically different approach to economic development that has been both a failure and a success.

Michigan

If Arizona presents a stark example of how state economic fortunes can deteriorate, Michigan provides a striking example of the opposite. As Arizona symbolized the Sunbelt, Michigan is the quintessential Rustbelt state. In the 1970s, the nation's economic ills were magnified in Michigan. The recessionary economy of this period had dire consequences for those industries upon which Michigan was highly dependent. During the late 1970s and early 1980s, the most vivid images of Michigan presented to the nation were of unemployed workers leaving the state to find employment. Many of these workers relocated to Texas. The auto industry lost over 100,000 jobs between 1978 and 1982. In this period the state's population, total employment, and personal income all declined relative to the national average. Michigan was one of the very first states to experience the threats posed by the new global economy: imported automobiles came to capture a larger and larger share of the domestic automobile market.

POLITICAL AND ECONOMIC TRADITIONS

Early History. The automobile shaped the twentieth century and dominated Michigan's political and economic development. John Jackson provides an interesting account of the path Michigan took to becoming the automobile capital of the world. The path has a rather remarkable beginning in the timber industry. In the nineteenth century, timber was the state's second largest industry behind agriculture. After the great fire, Michigan timber rebuilt much of Chicago. An extensive railroad network emerged in the state to ship lumber and the railroads came to have major influence in the state's politics and economy. With the abundance of lumber and transportation facilities, furniture manufacturing emerged as a major industry in the latter part of the nineteenth century. The timber industry also gave rise to the chemical industry when it was found that scrapwood could be used to evaporate brine brought out of salt wells. Eventually other byproducts from this process gave rise to the still visible chemical industry in the state.

At the turn of the century Michigan contained a set of diverse and successful industries. It was a state that had grown economically throughout the nineteenth century, first as the result of its bounty of valued resources, but later as the result of innovations and the creation of new industries. The automobile was not invented in Michigan. Indeed, the first commercial production of the auto in the United States was not even in Michigan. Yet the state's location and its diverse and innovative economy proved to be an excellent locale for the emer-

gent industry. Ransom Olds began commercial production of the automobile in 1899 and within fifteen years the state produced three-
quarters of the nation's automobiles. Jackson argues that the development of the automobile industry was the result of a simultaneous
combination of factors: the presence of entrepreneurs in the marine
engine business looking for new markets, existing industries, skilled
manufacturing workers, and the availability of local venture capital.[1]
Together, these factors provided the stimulus for continued innovation.

Michigan's economic development was not without considerable
conflict and tension. What was largely a rural backwater at the turn
of the century had been transformed into an industrial behemoth in
thirty years. In 1900, the three counties surrounding Detroit had a
total population of 426,000. In 1930 this same area had over 2 million
residents. Other auto producing cities like Flint and Lansing experienced similar growth during this period.

As the automobile industry and the state's population grew, relations between management and labor became increasingly tense. With
increased competition in the automobile industry, entrepreneurs like
Henry Ford, who had once assumed a paternalistic role concerning
the health and welfare of his workers, came to promote greater assembly line speeds and efficiency in the workplace and showed less
and less concern about worker morale or well-being. In some instances
the working conditions were tragic: at the Briggs and Stratton assembly plant, they calculated worker pay only when the assembly line
was moving. In the event that the assembly line stopped for any
reason, mechanical difficulties or otherwise, the clock for workers'
hourly wages also stopped until the line resumed operations.

These conditions provided fertile ground for the mobilization and
collective organization of labor. In 1937, the United Auto Workers
staged sit-down strikes at various plants and many confrontations
with management followed. Some of these confrontations, like the
famous battle of the overpass at the Ford Rouge plant, were very
bloody and served to rally workers to the cause of collective bargaining. The United Auto Workers eventually succeeded and this organization became a potent force in Michigan politics.

During World War II Michigan's factories became the "Arsenal of
Democracy." Wartime production needs stimulated even more growth
in the state's industrial capacity. With the financial support of the
United States government, huge facilities were built or converted by
the automobile industry to produce tanks, planes, and even boats.
After the war these facilities would be converted back to production
of automobiles and other consumer products. For the next twenty-

five years Michigan would flourish at the forefront of the industrial frontier.

The Post–World War II Era. At the end of the 1940s, after nearly a decade without domestic automobile production, there was tremendous demand for new cars. During the 1950s and 1960s the automobile industry grew, creating thousands of jobs building cars and in many support industries such as steel and rubber. These jobs had high wages and extensive benefits owing largely to the success of unions. Unions set the tone of Michigan politics well into the 1960s. The unions were not without their adversaries, however. Many outlying regions of the state resented the influence of the unions and served as a powerful competitive buffer within the state's politics. Thus, while the unions came to wield significant influence in post–World War II Michigan politics, conservative forces from the less industrialized western and northern parts of the state attenuated the influence of organized labor.

In the wake of the New Deal and World War II, the state leaned heavily in the Democratic direction. The coalition between the Democratic party and labor promoted policies that stimulated enormous growth in Michigan's public sector, placing it among the most activist states in the nation. By 1978 Michigan ranked 4th in the nation in terms of the adequacy of its AFDC grants.[2] The state ranked 6th in educational spending per pupil in 1977–78.[3] Numerous other indices could be supplied to make the same point. Michigan has a tradition that, by comparison with other states, marks it as one of the more interventionist in the post–World War II era.

While the Democratic party and labor were to set the tone for much of Michigan's post–World War II development, the partisan politics of the state remained competitive. In 1962 Republican George Romney was elected governor. He was succeeded by Republican William Milliken in 1968. While these Republicans were typically at variance with many of the details of the Democratic-labor coalition that had set the tone in the postwar era, neither of these governors sought to reduce the size of the public sector. Instead, these governors managed and maintained the extensive state bureaucracies. Michigan developed one of the nation's most comprehensive systems of higher education, and it also continued to be generous to its poor and unemployed.

The unwillingness of the Republican Romney and Milliken administrations to challenge far-reaching public commitments by Michigan government reflected a general consensus about the role of the state in Michigan. Labor remained powerful throughout most of this era. These Republican governors cooperated with Democratic coalitions in the legislature and the state's public sector continued to expand during this era. As the 1970s drew to a close, however, economic conditions threatened this long-standing consensus. Through the 1970s, Michigan had average personal incomes that were at least 10 percent above the national average. As the 1980s opened, new threats to the state's economy emerged that challenged this high standard of living.

A New Economic Era. In the 1970s signs emerged that Michigan's economy was faltering. Skyrocketing oil prices and changing tastes for automobiles, along with fierce foreign competition, ushered in a new era for the state. Domestic auto producers had always considered small cars as an auxiliary product, not taking them seriously. As oil prices climbed, many Americans were driven to purchase smaller, more economical foreign cars. For many, it was a permanent change as they found the fit and finish of these cars superior to that of domestically produced cars. The Big Three would begin a long slide that continues unabated to this day.

The recession of 1979 to 1982 hit hard, and Michigan was a state in crisis. The automobile-based economy began to experience even more extreme downturns. State unemployment levels reached 17 percent that year and many of the more automobile dependent localities began the 1980s experiencing the worst unemployment since the Great Depression. The government teetered ominously near default. In 1983, the state ran a $1.7 billion deficit despite across the board spending cuts. During this period, Michigan had the lowest bond rating of any state in the nation. Academic observers began to call for the diversification of the Michigan economy.[4]

The state's population dropped 2.3 percent in the 1980–83 period. Bookstores were swamped with demand for newspapers from the South and Southwest. U-Haul dealers complained of shortages of trailers and trucks as Michigan residents moved south, often to Texas, in pursuit of jobs. There were one-half million unemployed workers in Michigan in 1981, mostly from industries related to auto production. Houston, on the other hand, was creating jobs at the rate of 70,000 per year in the preceding five years. Northerners filled many of these positions and many of these émigrés were from Michigan.[5]

Many assumptions underlying the postwar consensus about the role and reach of the state began to be questioned as cycle after cycle of economic downturns plagued the state. Some blamed the state's fall from prosperity on government; some argued that the state's high taxes, unemployment insurance premiums, and workers' compensation had driven plants out of the state. Some blamed the leadership of the automobile industry: for too long, Detroit had relied on old designs, old production techniques, and hype to market its cars. With the oil crises of the 1970s, Americans began seeking more efficient cars. Detroit had ventured into small cars in the past—Corvair, Falcon, Pinto, Vega—but their efforts usually joined economical with "cheap." Imports, especially from Japan, became an attractive alternative to more and more Americans. These cars were economical and well-built. Suddenly the American automobile buyer became quality and economy conscious and an increasing portion of the American automobile market went to imports. Others contended that organized labor was the culprit. From this perspective, union success had caused Michigan's industries to fall from its competitive position because of rigid work rules and inflated wage demands made by the unions.

By commonly used measures the state's business environment fared poorly. For example, in rankings compiled by the Fantus Company (rankings that relied heavily on different state and local tax burdens), of the 48 contiguous states, Michigan ranked 45th.[6] In rankings compiled by the Alexander Grant Company in 1979, 1982, and 1984, Michigan was consistently last in business climate. Like the Fantus survey, the Grant Company rankings were heavily influenced by taxation, state regulated business, and labor costs.[7] By contrast, Texas ranked first in the Fantus study and 2 and 22 in the three Grant studies. Arizona ranked 15th in the Fantus study and between 5th and 29th in the three Grant studies.[8] It should be noted that while such rankings attract attention in economic development discussions, they are notoriously poor predictors of economic growth.[9]

Although some might argue that it was like closing the barn door after the cattle had escaped, the government of Michigan began to respond to some major signs of decline in the state's economy. Economic development policymaking emerged in the last years of William Milliken's administration. As noted above, Michigan's business climate was typically blamed for the condition of its economy. Responding to the Michigan Manufacturing Association, Milliken sought to reduce government-imposed cost disadvantages to business.

In 1981, Milliken proposed a major initiative to place Michigan at the forefront of technologically oriented production. Milliken created the Governor's High Technology Task Force in that same year, composed of representatives from the financial and academic communities. Working with this task force, Milliken emphasized both private and public investment to stimulate the state's high-technology industries. Milliken's early efforts departed from past practice in the state, where blue ribbon recommendations usually consisted of proposals to diversify the state's economy through recruiting outside firms. Within the new plans, Michigan's government was to assume a larger role in shaping its economy by actively supporting research centers, encouraging innovation, and providing capital for new firms.

In the midst of the economic crisis Democrat James Blanchard succeeded the retiring Milliken. He had a simple campaign theme that reflected the nature of the times: "Jobs, Jobs, Jobs." Blanchard assumed office as the Michigan economy was approaching its post-depression nadir. To cope with the $1.7 billion deficit, he cut spending and raised taxes, the latter being a very unpopular (if necessary) measure in an economic bust. With a Democratic majority in each house of the state legislature, Blanchard took the bold and politically risky move of raising the state's personal income tax. Because of the tax increase, a recall campaign against Blanchard and several state legislators dominated the early portion of his administration. While his popularity plummeted, Blanchard was not seriously threatened by the recall. This campaign did unseat two of Blanchard's legislative supporters in the Detroit area and the governor lost his majority in the legislature.

Michigan's fiscal crisis abated with the revenues produced by the tax increase and a turnaround in the automobile industry in 1985. Initially, Blanchard had followed the path set by his predecessor, William Milliken, and cut public expenditures. Blanchard cut another $225 million in his first year in office. However, with additional revenues provided by the tax increase and the economic recovery, Blanchard eventually restored public spending to its 1979 levels, targeting spending increases for public education, infrastructure, and economic development. After restoring spending levels he rolled back the tax increase before the 1986 election.

Blanchard created a Cabinet Council for Jobs and Economic Development with a primary goal of forming an economic development strategy. To do this, the council was to coordinate the economic development activities of the seven departments it represented as well as develop new programs that cut across departments. The council identified forestry, food products, and automobile suppliers as target industries developed from Blanchard's stated campaign goal of "Jobs, Jobs, Jobs." Perhaps more than anything else, the council succeeded in enforcing the governor's priorities by cutting through state bureaucratic resistance before being disbanded in late 1985.

Blanchard also brought representatives of industry and labor together to help the state formulate economic development strategies. He created the Governor's Commission on Jobs and Economic Development to serve as an advisory group. Originally, Blanchard had hoped that the commission would help to formulate strategies to promote innovation that could raise productivity and make the state's industries more competitive, especially in comparison to Japan. As John Jackson notes, however, the commission's operations typically reflected the private agendas of its membership. For example, instead of promoting innovation, a working group on automobile suppliers concentrated on traditional ways to reduce business costs. The commission, according to Jackson, served as a public forum for debating issues and managing the conflicts associated with traditional labor-management issues.[10] Conflict over the economic future of the state was managed, not removed. From the standpoint of private interests, this commission and the Entrepreneurial and Small Business Commission provided policy access for large and small business. From the standpoint of the government, these commissions helped to build supporting coalitions and legitimize policy proposals. They served the politically useful role of "getting one's ducks in a row" for promoting economic development policies.

These commissions were in some ways pragmatic, short-term responses to an economic crisis. The governor also sought to develop a long-range economic development strategy. To do this he quietly created a task force for long-term economic strategy at the Institute for Social Research at the University of Michigan. The task force was composed primarily of academics. They compiled "a research-based analysis of the state of the Michigan economy and some broad policy directives."[11] The report, entitled *The Path to Prosperity*, was released in 1984. The strategy presented in the study recognized the importance of government in nurturing the state's future economic development. The following basic themes were identified:

> Any economic development strategy must concentrate on the economic base, which in Michigan is primarily manufacturing and related business services;
>
> Michigan's future depends upon having innovative firms developing new products and production technologies;
>
> Private industry must take the lead in investing in these new technologies as government can only play a supportive role;
>
> State investments should be in education and research and in assistance to workers displaced by changing manufacturing technologies;
>
> State policies should concentrate more on the services valued by new and expanding businesses than on financial subsidies to relocating or failing firms;

Reduced state related business costs are not a quick fix solution to the development problem, but costs should be comparable to those of other states in the region.[12]

Rather than seeking simply to maintain existing industries, the task force underscored the importance of creating a productive environment that would stimulate innovation and new industry. Going into the mid-1980s, Michigan had experienced economic downturns, had attempted to systematically evaluate the problem, and engaged in a systematic strategy to stimulate its economy using the resources of the state to promote technical innovation. Unlike Arizona and Texas, where they viewed economic recovery in terms of changing external conditions, Michigan actively engaged in an attempt to modify the state's economic plight by intervening and modifying the productive environment.

New York

In "What New York Can Learn from Texas,"[13] an article with a title that betrays much of the conventional wisdom of the 1970s, New York compared very unfavorably with the then-burgeoning Texas economy. These comparisons help to highlight the plight of the state. New York's population had not grown since 1967 while that of Texas had increased 10 percent, largely because of steadily rising job opportunities in the private sector. Private nonagricultural employment in Texas had grown over 33 percent in the 1967–75 period while New York had suffered a 3.1 percent net loss in private employment. While per capita income was higher in New York than Texas, it was growing faster in Texas. In addition, New York was suffering annual losses in its manufacturing sector while Texas had enjoyed a net increase in the same period. Value added by manufacturing had risen twice as quickly in Texas as it had in New York.

This article attributed many of New York's economic problems to its public policies. For example, where Texas imposed no taxes on corporate profits or personal incomes, New York has had a tradition of high taxes; where Texas has had a right-to-work law, New York has reflected prolabor sentiments in a number of policy areas and unemployment benefits are much higher than those in Texas. The general conclusion reached by this less than sympathetic article was that New York should pay more attention to economic and business conditions. In addition, New York should capitalize on its natural and human capital, and on its massive investment in public education (80 percent of New York City high school graduates attend college).

POLITICAL AND ECONOMIC TRADITIONS

Early History. While the sentiments expressed in the above article are so typical that they have almost been elevated to the status of conventional wisdom, they miss a fundamental feature of New York's political-economic history. Perhaps more than any other state, New York State government has a long tradition of state intervention to promote economic development. Almost from its inception, New York State government operated to create an institutional framework that was conducive to economic growth and private enterprise. Through its development of law and the legislative and judicial interpretation of property rights, the state created a predictable and stable legal-economic environment.

Beyond the legal order it established, New York State also engaged directly in activities to stimulate its economy. New York State government distributed "public largess" directly to individuals, groups, or communities.[14] The state aided private enterprise engaging in what were deemed desirable forms of agriculture, manufacturing, or transport through bounties, grants, or subsidies.[15] The state also invested its funds in private enterprises and made loans. Beyond financial aid, the state provided legal incentives to promote certain forms of economic activity. For example, one early law in the state gave tax exemptions to producers of wool, cotton, and linen.[16] The state also developed the corporate charter as a mechanism to grant special privileges, legal or otherwise, to individuals or groups engaged in activities the state deemed desirable. Under the rubric of the public interest these charters would give firms powers of eminent domain or authority to set and collect tolls. In this early era corporate activity was largely for public purposes. The state also regulated business to foster particular economic goals.

The best known example of New York's involvement in its economy is the construction of the Erie Canal. According to one historian, the decision to build the Erie Canal constituted a major turning point in the state's involvement in its economy.[17] This endeavor increased the state's direct expenditures in transportation by almost 100 fold in a period of roughly thirty years. By providing access to markets, the canal touched off an economic boom that was felt both inside and outside the state. The success of the canal also stimulated canal construction in other states.

The involvement of the state of New York in its economy, and the power of state government, would recede by the middle of the nineteenth century. New York government, powerful by the standards of the day, had the political capacity to incur debt to build canals and finance other major public undertakings. Yet, while quite powerful, the permeability of the political processes of New York State government increased as the power of the private sector rose. New York's government came increasingly to serve as a distributive arena. Newly powerful private organizations, more than markets or constituents, came to influence the allocation of public projects. Gunn observes that those who benefited most from public projects and economic growth were the least willing to finance it through taxes. Groups representing geographical or commercial interests would converge on the state legislature and succeed in obtaining special concessions or public works projects and avoid bearing the costs associated with these policies. The legislature was ill-suited to manage or control these interests but instead conceded to many such demands. The result was a fiscal crisis. The ultimate response to this crisis was a reform of New York's government. While the government's inability to manage and control powerful interests converging on the capitol was at the heart of the problem, by and large the central premise of these reforms was that the fiscal crisis in New York resulted because New York State government was *too* powerful. The ensuing reforms greatly weakened the power of the legislature, particularly in fiscal matters. For the most part, New York government would retreat from economic intervention for the remainder of the century.

New York entered the twentieth century as a commercial and industrial giant, leading the nation in its prosperous path through the Industrial Revolution. State intervention in this era was minimal. All of this was shaken by the Crash of 1929 and the ensuing depression. In the wake of the Great Depression New York supplemented federal action and established its own Department of Commerce to attempt to address the economic crisis.

The Post–World War II Era. Following World War II, New York's Department of Commerce focused on making structural adjustments to adapt to the postwar economy. The Department of Commerce emphasized the importance of the multiplier effect on manufacturing jobs. Consequently, for much of the postwar period, New York's efforts in economic development focused on stimulating the state's manufacturing sector as a means to promote employment. The Job Development Authority was created to provide long-term, low-interest fixed asset loans to manufacturers to promote employment.

As for most states, the 1950s were prosperous years for New York.

This prosperity showed signs of faltering in New York quite early, however. While Arizona, Texas, and even Michigan were basking in the growth of the 1960s, New York's manufacturing sector began to suffer decline. To stem this tide, New York began using tax preferences in its economic development efforts. Most of these tax preferences emphasized manufacturing. In 1963 the state allowed business to use a "double depreciation" to write off investments in buildings, machinery, and equipment used in goods-producing activities. In 1968, the state established an Urban Job Incentive Program that provided even more extensive tax breaks to create jobs in inner city areas.

Despite these efforts, manufacturing continued to decline in New York and many state leaders began to search for an explanation. In addition, by the end of the 1960s the state's industrial mix had become concentrated in those manufacturing areas that were declining fastest. The state lost over 500,000 manufacturing jobs between 1968 and 1985.[18] In a perverse form of Darwinian evolution, the state's tax incentives probably forestalled the demise of some unproductive manufacturing sectors, did little to abate the trend in manufacturing decline generally, and also did little to ensure the long-term economic health of the state.

A New Economic Era. In the early 1970s, New York lost over 600,000 jobs and by the mid-1970s growth in per capita personal income ranked 50th in the nation. At the same time, New York was bearing the burden of the expansive spending policies initiated under Nelson Rockefeller. As the national economy slid into a recession in the mid-seventies, New York City bordered on financial insolvency and the state was in little better shape.

In the midst of the state's fiscal crisis, a comprehensive economic development strategy was formulated in the mid 1970s. Initiated by the state, a "dialectic" between the state and the business community emerged in the late 1970s.[19] Faced with a very bleak economy, New York government began formulating and implementing comprehensive programs to stimulate recovery. These programs sought to evaluate both the costs and apparent benefits of government policies. The state financed research, risks and investments, shared costs of developing export markets, and financed job training and education. Through these acts, the state hoped to reduce the short-term costs of capital and labor and thereby enhance the productive environment of the state over the long run. The government sought to promote growth through higher employment and high wages. To do this, the state became an integral part of the economy and reorganized its productive environment, promoting growth while attempting to eliminate the inequities that markets normally produce. As Magid observes, New York sought to promote growth with equity.[20]

In June 1978 Governor Hugh Carey established the Economic Affairs Cabinet. Its mission was to define and implement economic development strategies and projects. In August of the same year, the High Technology Opportunities Work Force Advisory Council was created, which proposed the revitalization of the New York State Science and Technology Foundation, newly endowed by the legislature in 1981. This foundation was given power to designate Centers for Advanced Technology within the state. The foundation also authorized the New York Urban Development Corporation and a Center for Industrial Innovation at Rensselaer Polytechnic Institute.

Governor Carey presented an economic development plan entitled "Targets of Economic Opportunity: A Strategy for Economic Development in New York State" in July 1979.[21] The plan sought to strengthen state efforts to identify growth industries within the state. In a departure from past practice, which provided incentives to all industries loosely defined as involved as manufacturing, Carey called for identifying priorities and targeting efforts.

Specialized efforts to promote economic development proliferated in New York. Aid in the form of direct grants and loans was made available. The government also sought to reduce the costs of production directly and indirectly within its control, through reducing taxes or costs of land or energy. In addition, the government subsidized specialized job training to reduce costs to employers. Sometimes the state paid wages while workers were in training. The state also provided services that could increase the productivity of business, lower its costs, or both. This normally took the form of constructing rail sidings or extending access roads for a particular company's use.

When he entered office in 1982 Mario Cuomo confronted a fiscal crisis. The state faced a $1.8 billion deficit. In this and ensuing years Cuomo and the legislature would hammer out compromises that blended fiscal moderation tempered by commitment to traditional Democratic goals. After a tax increase in his first year, he subsequently succeeded in reducing taxes by roughly 1 percent of the state's annual budget. As New York's economy began to surge toward the end of his first term, Cuomo was blessed with rapidly increasing revenues producing budget surpluses.

In 1984 Cuomo issued an executive order creating an Industrial Cooperation Council (ICC). Intended to provide a coordinated approach to economic development, the council was composed of representatives of labor, business, and the academic communities. The ICC defined distress in terms of dropping employment and production resulting from import penetration and decreasing productivity. Job loss was targeted as the most important feature of economic decline and efforts were made to find new jobs for dislocated workers at wages comparable to those they had been earning. The Industrial Cooperation Council helped negotiate a compact between the state's largest business organizations and the AFL-CIO that affirmed a series of principles for cooperation to confront the problems caused by structural unemployment.

Cuomo's efforts in economic development were more successful in his second term. Most of the success was administrative. Cuomo had appointed an economic development "czar" in his first term. This czar, Vincent Tese, began to make headway in reorganizing and rationalizing the state's enormous economic development system.

In 1987 the state passed the Omnibus Economic Development Act that changed the previously mentioned Department of Commerce to the Department of Economic Development. Acknowledging the challenging economic context that confronted the state, the act recognized a need for the ability to provide coordinated and comprehensive economic development assistance. This legislation articulated the state's economic development strategy:

> It is in the public interest for the state to promote the general welfare and prosperity of its citizens through a comprehensive effort to ensure the state's economic future, including efforts to reverse economic stagnation and decline in certain industrial sectors and regions and localities; to stimulate new productivity and competitiveness of existing industries; to encourage the start-up of new businesses and the expansion of existing firms; to provide new economic and employment opportunities for the state's citizens; to ensure an adequate supply of skilled labor to meet the needs of an expanding economy; and to provide for advanced scientific research that can be of significant value to the state's economy.[22]

This act integrated and coordinated the state's economic development apparatus to streamline the delivery of economic development assistance. Among the various programs the act established a network of regional offices that provided customized services for each state region, funding for technical and financial assistance to manufacturing firms, an economic development training skills program, and an industrial infrastructure program.

Remarkably, by the end of the 1980s New York State government had returned to its early nineteenth-century posture of economic activism. Using the public interest as a justification, the state now nurtured economic activities deemed to be socially desirable by creating legal incentives and financial rewards. The state would experience economic resurgence in the late 1980s with growth in manufacturing, nonagricultural employment, and personal income.

This examination of New York began by reflecting on an article from the 1970s entitled "What New York Can Learn from Texas." It is fitting that we end our consideration by examining a much more recent article entitled "Sunbelt's Future: Lessons from Up North?"[23] The article quotes Dallas economist Bernard Weinstein: "Many parts of the Frost-belt are returning to prosperity, while the Sunbelt has collapsed into only a few 'sunspots.' "[24] The South, according to the article, has neglected to invest in its human capital, with education programs being among the stingiest in the nation. The article notes: "But now it turns out that a balanced tax system and education and social expenditures—all traditionally anathema to the Texas legislature—are not the fruit of pointy headed Yankee liberal thinking, but rather the basics of running a resourceful and resilient society."[25]

Pursuing Self-sustained Growth in Two Interventionist States

Michigan and New York exemplify the plight of many economically and politically mature states with well-developed industrial bases and extensive public sectors. For much of the post–World War II era, these developed economic and political sectors appeared to serve as brakes on their growth, as expansion occurred more rapidly in the less developed states. These states were among the first to experience economic decline in the post–World War II era and in both political leadership emerged that promoted programmatic efforts to try to stimulate their economies. Instead of slashing state taxes or providing huge incentives to lure industries, these efforts emphasized the role of the state in creating environments that could stimulate economic growth. The emphasis was not just on jobs but on higher paying jobs.

From this survey of four states we can see that states are differentially responsive to external economic conditions. The performance of a state's economy, its economic development strategy, and the seeming success or failure of that strategy is, to a large degree, determined outside its boundaries by forces at work in the nation's economy. What succeeded in one era failed in another, and what appeared as a failure initially appeared to be beneficial in another context. To understand the reality of state economic performance, we must better understand the effects of context on state economies and isolate the economies of states from the national economy.

CHAPTER 5

Context: Isolating the Economies of States

> *The reason we still have 25 percent unemployment in parts of the Arkansas delta is not because I don't work 60 hours a week . . . it's because of national political policies and international economics that I can't do anything about.*
>
> William Clinton
> Governor of Arkansas

Governor Clinton's comment draws attention to a fundamental but often overlooked aspect of state economies. Lawmakers, citizens, journalists, employees, and employers focus on state policies believed to influence state economic performance, yet they seldom consider their state's economic performance in the broader context of the national economy. States are not autonomous economic entities and state economies are not blank slates on which policymakers can write. Instead, they exist as part of a national economy, itself influenced by the global economy. Even the most aggressive state efforts to stimulate their economies could not be expected to offset large national economic patterns.

The study of state political economy is difficult because these economies are very open and thus states and their economies are like moving targets. One state may act and nothing happens, another state may do nothing and experience dramatic change. This volatility is due largely to the influence of the nation's economic performance on a state's economic vitality. The relative pervasiveness of the nation's economy influences the context in which state political economy unfolds. As could be seen in the survey of state histories, in some eras great energy went into efforts to nurture economic development, while in others economic growth could be taken for granted.

This chapter focuses on two distinct but related sets of questions that should help to pin down the nature of state-level influence on state economies. First, how dependent are states on the national economy, how do individual states vary in their responsiveness to national economic fluctuations, and what is the nature of state economic performance independent of national trends? Understanding this dependence can provide a more refined picture of the degree of opportunity states have to influence their economic performance and the actual nature of state economic performance when the pervasive influence of the nation's economy is stripped away. Second, is the relationship between state and national economies getting stronger or weaker, are states becoming more or less dominated by national-level economic forces, and has the economic context of the states changed?

The Dependence of States on the National Economy

Interest centers on two aspects of state economic performance: the *dependence* of state economies on the national economy and the *underlying performance* of state economies, independent of the nation's economic fortunes. From these two dimensions, four basic patterns of dependence can be envisioned, each of which defines a dramatically different economic context.

If dominated completely by national economic fluctuations, change in the nation's economy would be mirrored by an equal change in a state's economy. In such states it seems unlikely that state-level phenomena would have any unique effect on state economic performance. Alternatively, some states may exhibit a looser connection to national fortunes. For example, a state might experience only a portion of the nation's economic change, growing more slowly during booms but also suffering less severely during recessions. Such a state could be characterized as relatively independent.

It is also possible that a state might exhibit an inverse relationship to the nation's economy. Employment growth, for example, might slow in some states as a function of employment growth for the nation as a whole because such national growth might stem the tide of jobs to a less developed economy. Such states also might gain in employment when national growth in jobs is declining because of comparative cost advantages in these states. Each of these alternative scenarios will be analyzed in detail below.

Once we take the performance of the nation's economy into account, we may ask how well a state is performing economically over time. Is a state growing or declining once national economic fluctuations are controlled? Failure to consider the national economy's influence on a state's growth could lead to a distorted picture of a state's actual economic trends. Imagine two states, one with comparatively low annual growth and another with comparatively high annual growth. The former state could be relatively independent from the nation's economy and experience only a fraction of its annual economic changes. Yet, independent of these nationally driven changes, this state may turn in significant annual gains in economic growth. The other state may grow at a heightened rate as a function of the nation's economic growth but, with these national effects controlled, there may be no underlying trend of growth or even a pattern of significant decline. First impressions would tell us that the former state was suffering and the latter succeeding. Closer inspection, taking the impact of the national economy into account, would provide *exactly the opposite conclusion*. It is thus essential that economies of nation and state be evaluated.

EVALUATING NATIONAL DEPENDENCE AND STATE TRENDS

Evaluating states' dependence on the nation's economy and their underlying economic health is a simple matter. Economic change in each state may be modeled as a function of national economic change and time, where time captures any underlying trend in a state's economy, independent of the nation's economic performance. Stated more formally:

$$\text{State Economy}_t = a + b_1 \text{ National Economy}_t + b_2 \text{ Year}_t + e_t,$$

where, in addition to the intercept a and error term e, State Economy$_t$ equals the annual percentage of change in a state's economic indicator, National Economy$_t$ equals the national change in that economic indicator and Year$_t$ equals 1968 to 1989, a is the intercept. Estimation of this simple model provides coefficients with useful analytical characteristics. The coefficient b_1 describes the character of the state's relationship to the nation's economy. Statistically, the coefficient may be significant indicating a pattern of close covariation. Alternatively, the coefficient may not be statistically significant, indicating that fluctuations in the nation's economy are not tightly tied to those in a given state. Substantively the coefficient reveals the nature of the nation's impact on a state. The coefficient can be interpreted in terms of its absolute value. A coefficient less than one would show that a state experiences changes that are only a proportion of national changes. A coefficient greater than one would reveal that a state changed disproportionately in relation to national economic changes, growing rapidly during prosperous periods but suffering severely during national recessions. Finally, this coefficient may be interpreted in terms of its sign. Some states may benefit from national downturns and others hurt during national economic expansion.

Coefficient b_2 also yields simple interpretation and aids in classifying the states. If this coefficient is less than zero, it would indicate that a state was suffering underlying economic decline, when the effects of the nation's economy are controlled. When this coefficient is greater than zero, a state has an underlying growth trend, independent of the nation's economy. The two coefficients thus provide two categories each, yielding a two-by-two scheme for considering the states, as seen in Table 3.

TABLE 3. Classification of States according to Growth Rates and National Influence

		National Impact	
		Independent	Dependent
	Growth	Autonomous-Growing	Dependent-Growing
State Level Trend			
	Decline	Autonomous-Declining	Dependent-Declining

In the analysis that follows, the simple model outlined in Table 3 is applied to three different measures of economic performance: per capita personal income, nonagricultural employment, and value added by manufacturing. The states will be classified according to their dependence on the nation's economy, and their underlying economic performance (see Appendix A for a discussion of data and measurement, and Appendix B for a discussion of methodology).

Per Capita Personal Income. Table 4 presents the results of analyzing annual changes in per capita personal income. Examination of R^2 reveals that the performance of the model varies widely among the states, from accounting for almost none of the variation in North Dakota to over 90 percent of the variation in Pennsylvania. Generally, the model does well in most of the states. In all but a few instances (Iowa, Oklahoma, North Dakota, Rhode Island, South Dakota, and

Wyoming), the nation's economy exerted a statistically significant influence on each state's economy. The magnitude of this impact varied widely between the states. At one extreme are states like Indiana, Arkansas, and Michigan, each of which experienced an estimated 150 percent or more of the changes experienced at the national level. At the other extreme are South Dakota, Rhode Island, and Iowa that experienced only a small fraction of national-level changes. Clearly, on this economic indicator states differ dramatically in their sensitivity to fluctuations in the national economy.

The states also display a variety of underlying growth trends. Roughly half the states have a statistically significant underlying trend in personal income. On the other hand, about half the states displayed no statistically discernable trend in personal income growth independent of the national trend. For these states, changes in per capita personal income were almost strictly the result of national trends.

Substantively, the states vary widely in the direction and magnitude of their underlying trends. At one extreme are declining states such as Wyoming and Louisiana that had significant negative trends in per capita personal income.[1] Many southern and western states that normally are characterized as part of the Sunbelt, such as Texas, Colorado, Arizona, Alabama, and South Carolina, suffered net decline in per capita personal income when the effects of the national economy are held constant. At the other extreme are states that had underlying trends of growth. Here, many states of the Rustbelt and Northeast experienced significant growth in per capita personal income.

It is interesting how well Rustbelt and northeastern states fare in this analysis. The 1980s witnessed some dramatic turnarounds in the economic performance of many states, particularly New Hampshire, Massachusetts, Connecticut, New York, and New Jersey. The analysis here, using data reaching back to the 1960s, reveals that these states had strong economic foundations long before the 1980s.

Table 5 categorizes the states according to their responsiveness to national economic performance and their underlying trend. Complementing our discussion to this point, this table also makes clear that things are not always as they seem. First, looking at the dependent-declining category, many states that could serve as models for those extolling limited economic intervention are present. Most notably for this analysis, Arizona falls into this category. It is a state that would not have grown if not for national economic growth. The political economy of this state, we may safely surmise, failed to create conditions that would allow the state to withstand bad national economic conditions.

In the independent-declining category are states that experienced

TABLE 4. Annual Change in Per Capita Personal Income by State, 1968–1989: The Effects of the National Economy and State Trends

State	Constant B_0	National Economy B_1	t	State Trend (B_2)	t	Adj. R^2
Alabama	181.95	1.22	13.29	−0.09	−2.59	.90
Arizona	167.76	1.19	7.98	−0.08	−1.47	.76
Arkansas	304.68	1.58	10.58	−0.15	2.67	.85
California	−112.71	0.87	8.05	0.05	1.37	.75
Colorado	125.86	0.67	5.19	−0.06	−1.27	.57
Connecticut	−404.08	0.66	4.25	0.20	3.44	.55
Delaware	−101.46	1.09	5.86	0.05	0.71	.61
Florida	14.78	1.28	8.79	−0.01	−0.13	.78
Georgia	−6.85	1.24	9.18	0.00	0.01	.80
Idaho	111.37	1.21	3.69	−0.05	−0.45	.36
Illinois	−108.55	1.04	8.85	0.05	1.20	.78
Indiana	−112.42	1.61	11.17	0.06	1.00	.85
Iowa	95.40	0.51	1.71	−0.05	−0.41	.05
Kansas	210.44	1.14	4.85	−0.11	−1.17	.53
Kentucky	108.51	1.27	7.82	−0.05	−0.88	.74
Louisiana	340.31	0.53	2.81	−0.17	−2.35	.37
Maine	−300.50	0.91	4.97	0.15	2.16	.55
Maryland	−156.33	0.67	2.91	0.08	0.90	.25
Massachusetts	−270.66	0.89	4.73	0.14	1.89	.52
Michigan	−27.87	1.54	11.54	0.01	0.26	.87
Minnesota	−14.52	1.26	6.38	0.01	0.09	.65
Mississippi	288.19	1.37	9.39	−0.14	−2.60	.82
Missouri	−51.61	1.04	3.17	0.02	0.21	.28
Montana	48.37	1.28	6.57	−0.02	−0.33	.66
Nebraska	172.14	1.01	3.50	−0.08	−0.78	.35
Nevada	−101.16	1.14	6.81	0.05	0.79	.68
New Hampshire	−432.75	1.34	5.47	0.22	2.33	.60
New Jersey	−341.53	0.81	3.17	0.17	1.75	.33
New Mexico	159.61	0.80	3.78	−0.08	−0.98	.40
New York	−303.34	0.64	4.24	0.15	2.62	.51
North Carolina	32.68	1.44	13.29	−0.01	−0.40	.89
North Dakota	501.83	0.59	0.98	−0.25	−1.09	.01
Ohio	21.81	1.10	13.36	−0.01	−0.36	.89
Oklahoma	325.58	0.59	2.14	−0.16	−1.54	.20
Oregon	−12.65	1.29	11.61	0.01	0.14	.86
Pennsylvania	−63.91	0.90	15.24	0.03	1.42	.92
Rhode Island	−213.58	0.38	1.62	0.11	1.21	.08
South Carolina	182.03	1.32	7.84	−0.09	−1.42	.75
South Dakota	81.30	0.26	0.51	−0.04	−0.21	.00
Tennessee	68.59	1.31	10.45	−0.03	−0.72	.84
Texas	274.17	0.90	4.12	−0.14	−1.65	.47
Utah	55.57	0.99	7.07	−0.03	−0.52	.70
Vermont	−299.27	0.93	6.11	0.15	2.58	.65
Virginia	−16.46	1.14	12.15	0.01	0.23	.87
Washington	−42.77	1.06	6.28	0.02	0.33	.64
West Virginia	341.63	0.84	4.11	−0.17	−2.19	.50
Wisconsin	−76.63	0.92	8.10	0.00	0.88	.75
Wyoming	483.88	0.53	1.30	−0.24	−1.56	.10

Note: Data used in analyses are described in Appendix A.
$t \geqslant |1.72|$ significant at $\alpha = .10$: two-tailed test.
$t \geqslant |2.07|$ significant at $\alpha = .05$: two-tailed test.
$t \geqslant |2.82|$ significant at $\alpha = .01$: two-tailed test.

TABLE 5. Personal Income: Classification of States according to Responsiveness to the National Economy and State-Level Economic Trends

		Correspondence to National Economic Fluctuations	
		Relatively Independent	Relatively Dependent
State-Level Trend	Growth	CA, CT, GA, ME, MD, MA, NJ, NY, PA, RI, VT, WI	DE, IL, IN, MI, MN, MO, NV, NH, OR, VA, WA
	Decline	CO, IA, KS, LA, NM, ND, OK, SD, TX, UT, WV, WY	AL, AZ, AR, FL, ID, KY, MS, MT, NB, NC, OH, SC, TN

Note: Data used in analyses are described in Appendix A.

only a proportion of the nation's economic change and that were characterized by declining growth independent of the nation's economy. It is noteworthy that Texas falls into this category. The state experienced roughly 90 percent of the nation's changes in per capita personal income and thus is relatively independent from the nation's economy. Unfortunately for Texans, the analysis shows that the state suffered a mild but statistically significant trend of decline in per capita personal income independent of the nation's economy. Like Arizona, Texas was a state that would not have experienced growth in personal income in the absence of growth at the national level.

In the dependent-growing category are states where the impact of the national economy was magnified but also was characterized by underlying trends of growth in per capita personal income. Notably, Michigan falls into this category. It is often said in Michigan that when the nation's economy coughs, Michigan get pneumonia. This is evident in the estimated impact of national changes in personal income on change in Michigan: a 1 percent change nationally would translate into a 1.54 percent change in Michigan. This would not be a revelation to policymakers or residents in the state. Automobile sales are tightly bound to the health of the nation's economy. When national booms can stimulate comparatively huge demand for new cars, Michigan's economy flourishes. National recessions, however, can translate into depression era levels of unemployment as automakers close down plants in response to declining demand. Michigan also displays a slight positive state trend in per capita personal income, although this trend is not statistically significant. For the most part, change in per capita personal income in Michigan is dominated by the performance of the national economy.

The last category contains states classified as independent-growing. New York falls into this category. For the period studied, New York experienced only an estimated 64 percent of national changes in per capita personal income and thus was relatively autonomous. Underlying this, however, was a strong and statistically significant trend of growth in per capita personal income. This suggests that while the national economy might wax and wane, per capita personal income in New York continued upward at a significant rate.

Overall, this simple analysis of per capita personal income reveals that collectively the states are, for the most part, highly tied to the nation's economic performance: it was the rare state with a pattern of growth in personal income that was not tied significantly to national changes. Substantively, however, the nature of the ties that bind states to the nation's performance in personal income growth reveals interesting differences. Most notably Table 5, which summarizes these patterns, makes clear that things are not always what they seem. Many states that were success stories in the 1960s and 1970s benefited disproportionately from the national economy. In terms of trends within their states independent of the national economy, there is little to applaud. On the other hand, some supposed declining giants of the 1960s and 1970s were in reality less tied to the nation's economy. Many of these states provide evidence of state-level growth independent of national fortunes.

Nonagricultural Employment. Table 6 presents the results of analyzing annual changes in levels of nonagricultural employment in the states as a function of national changes and state-level trends. The most notable feature of this analysis, in comparison to the results from analyzing per capita personal income, is how little of the variation in employment growth is captured by these models. For the most part, national changes and state-level trends account for almost none of the changes in employment growth experienced annually by the states.

Some states benefited from growth in employment at the national level while others were harmed by this growth, although the effects of national change are only occasionally significant. For example, Vermont, Connecticut, and Alabama rank comparatively highly in terms of the positive impact of national employment growth, although in none of these cases is the impact of national growth statistically significant. States such as Kansas, Missouri, Arizona, Pennsylvania, New Jersey, and Nebraska all suffered because of growth in national employment, and this effect was statistically significant ($p = .1$). National

TABLE 6. Annual Change in Nonagricultural Employment by State, 1968–1989: The Effects of the National Economy and State Trends

State	Constant B_0	National Economy B_1	t	State Trend (B_2)	t	Adj. R^2
Alabama	196.67	0.650	2.18	−0.090	−1.13	.16
Arizona	6.24	−0.580	−1.58	0.000	−0.001	.02
Arkansas	−48.80	0.570	1.46	0.020	0.22	.01
California	−202.50	0.130	0.30	0.100	0.79	.00
Colorado	−102.84	−0.410	−1.24	0.050	0.56	.00
Connecticut	−10.36	0.740	1.06	0.006	0.03	.00
Delaware	459.53	−0.238	−0.72	−0.230	−2.51	.19
Florida	−122.12	0.318	0.47	0.060	0.32	.00
Georgia	−171.86	0.328	1.16	0.087	1.07	.02
Idaho	90.73	−0.169	−0.45	−0.439	−0.41	.00
Illinois	−90.59	0.234	0.63	0.047	0.44	.00
Indiana	202.49	0.067	0.24	−0.100	−1.22	.00
Iowa	216.16	0.146	0.54	−0.107	−1.37	.07
Kansas	104.41	−1.810	−1.86	−0.048	−0.17	.07
Kentucky	239.23	0.172	0.46	−0.119	−1.12	.00
Louisiana	−374.10	−0.006	−0.02	0.190	1.97	.08
Maine	110.66	−0.101	−0.24	−0.053	−0.45	.00
Maryland	−513.29	−0.392	−0.53	0.261	1.22	.00
Massachusetts	193.33	−0.177	−0.49	−0.096	−0.92	.00
Michigan	−46.14	0.180	0.48	0.025	0.22	.01
Minnesota	−35.72	−0.155	−0.41	0.019	0.18	.00
Mississippi	−136.48	0.400	1.02	0.069	0.64	.00
Missouri	−197.76	−0.693	−1.79	0.102	0.92	.09
Montana	216.64	0.374	0.72	−0.109	−0.73	.00
Nebraska	60.71	−0.493	−1.47	−0.028	−0.30	.01
Nevada	−119.08	0.377	0.94	0.061	0.52	.00
New Hampshire	22.07	0.070	0.18	−0.010	−0.09	.00
New Jersey	−115.75	−0.509	−1.83	0.060	0.76	.08
New Mexico	−200.77	−0.122	−0.48	0.103	1.40	.01
New York	106.66	−0.031	−0.09	0.055	0.60	.00
North Carolina	92.31	−0.415	−1.28	−0.040	−0.48	.00
North Dakota	67.11	0.358	0.83	−0.030	−0.26	.00
Ohio	66.88	0.206	0.55	−0.030	−0.31	.00
Oklahoma	−297.56	0.517	1.34	0.151	1.36	.07
Oregon	152.04	0.454	1.36	−0.070	−0.78	.02
Pennsylvania	96.83	−0.520	−1.46	−0.047	−0.46	.02
Rhode Island	−288.84	−0.165	−0.52	0.147	1.64	.04
South Carolina	109.37	0.060	0.14	−0.050	−0.43	.00
South Dakota	94.79	0.476	1.42	−0.040	−0.48	.01
Tennessee	−100.66	0.138	0.36	0.051	0.47	.00
Texas	120.12	0.032	0.08	−0.059	−0.51	.00
Utah	199.16	0.009	0.03	−0.100	−1.12	.00
Vermont	157.91	1.005	4.14	−0.080	−1.13	.44
Virginia	−196.47	0.020	0.08	0.100	1.34	.00
Washington	466.67	−0.022	−0.04	−0.230	−1.67	.04
West Virginia	−78.09	−0.190	−0.57	0.040	0.43	.00
Wisconsin	116.19	0.619	1.83	−0.058	−0.60	.07
Wyoming	−141.55	0.234	−0.90	0.073	0.97	.00

Note: Data used in analyses are described in Appendix A.
$t \geq |1.72|$ significant at α = .10: two-tailed test.
$t \geq |2.07|$ significant at α = .05: two-tailed test.
$t \geq |2.82|$ significant at α = .01: two-tailed test.

expansion of employment, it would appear, may retard employment growth in these states as workers are drawn away to other parts of the country.

State-level trends in employment growth, independent of the national trends, are only rarely significant in the statistical sense. With national trends controlled Delaware and Washington suffered significant decline in growth in employment, while Louisiana and Rhode Island had positive and significant trends in employment growth.

States are categorized according to the impact of national change and their underlying state trends in Table 7. As noted above, growth in employment was only rarely tied significantly to national changes in employment growth. Substantively, however, national growth stimulated growth in employment in some states while others suffered from national growth. Hence, Table 7 classifies states according to whether national employment growth had a positive or negative impact on state employment growth. The table also classifies states according to whether they had underlying trends of growth or decline in employment with the effects of national changes held constant. These results must be taken with a very high degree of caution, however, because very few of the relationships are statistically significant. Changing levels of employment, it would appear, occur in a sporadic fashion, at least compared to growth in per capita personal income. Decisions concerning plant relocation, construction, or opening may be tied only loosely to the performance of the nation's economy. Furthermore, employment growth in states may be tied to complex patterns of demographic change and regional migration of population. The diffusion of technology and production practices to a state with lower labor costs might stimulate employment in one state, while a new technological innovation or product might stimulate

TABLE 7. Nonagricultural Employment: Classification of States according to Responsiveness to the National Economy and State-Level Economic Trends

		Correspondence to National Economic Fluctuations	
		Relatively Independent	Relatively Dependent
State-Level Trend	Growth	AR, CA, CT, FL, GA, IL, MI, MS, NV, OK, TN, VA	AZ, CO, LA, MD, MN, MO, NJ, NM, NY, RI, WV, WY
	Decline	AL, IN, IA, KY, MT, NH, ND, OR, SC, SD, TX, UT, VT, WI	DE, ID, KS, ME, MA, NB, NC, PA, WA

Note: Data used in analyses are described in Appendix A.

employment in a state with higher labor and production costs. Perhaps the most important lesson to be learned from the analysis of changing employment levels is that it is not highly patterned and is instead likely the result of a myriad of decisions and forces.

Value Added by Manufacturing. Table 8 presents the results of analyzing change in value added by manufacturing. It shows that, like per capita personal income, the model does quite well here, capturing roughly three-quarters of the variation in growth in this indicator in several states and at least half the variation in many states. There are, however, some states in which the model does poorly, indicating that neither national patterns of manufacturing change nor state-level trends exerted much influence on growth in value added by manufacturing. In states such as Arizona, Arkansas, Louisiana, Montana, New Mexico, Oklahoma, Texas, Vermont, Washington, and Wyoming the model accounts for less than 10 percent of the variation in changes in value added by manufacturing.

Like changes in per capita personal income, most states felt national-level fluctuations in value added by manufacturing. National-level changes in this indicator had a statistically significant effect on changes in the vast majority of the states. Substantively, the impact is large for many states. Often, a 1 percent change in value added in manufacturing at the national level had a magnified impact at the state level. A handful of states experienced growth that was only proportionate to the national-level change. In only one state, Delaware, was national-level growth associated with decline and this result is not statistically significant.

Only seven states exhibit trends in value added by manufacturing that are statistically significant ($p = .1$). The estimated trends divide the states rather neatly into categories of winners and losers. New Hampshire, Georgia, and Connecticut had positive and significant trends in value added by manufacturing independent of national fluctuations. Alternatively, Oklahoma was characterized by a significant negative trend in change in this economic indicator.

Table 9 summarizes the general impact of national change and state trends in value added by classifying the states into four categories. As this table makes clear, almost all the states can be considered dependent on national changes in manufacturing. In only seven states was the impact of change at the national level less than unity. These states, also, were characterized by declining trends at the state level. It is interesting that Texas falls into this category. The agricultural and resource orientation of the state may have kept it from expanding its manufacturing base during this period, at least relative to other states.

TABLE 8. Annual Change in Value Added by Manufacturing by State, 1968–1987:
The Effects of the National Economy and State Trends

State	Constant B_0	National Economy B_1	t	State Trend (B_2)	t	Adj. R^2
Alabama	−301.17	1.790	4.75	0.15	0.91	.52
Arizona	710.12	0.920	0.60	−0.35	−0.52	.00
Arkansas	724.82	3.820	1.92	−0.37	−0.41	.09
California	651.22	1.830	2.38	−0.33	−0.96	.21
Colorado	161.46	1.120	2.92	−0.08	−0.47	.27
Connecticut	−565.24	1.560	3.47	0.28	1.42	.38
Delaware	460.86	−0.010	−0.06	−0.23	−2.48	.16
Florida	−194.40	1.410	2.98	0.10	0.47	.27
Georgia	−610.34	1.630	4.20	0.31	1.79	.49
Idaho	341.30	1.940	2.77	−0.17	−0.55	.25
Illinois	−2.98	1.870	6.05	−0.0003	0.00	.65
Indiana	−188.12	2.980	6.98	0.09	0.50	.71
Iowa	540.90	1.420	3.75	−0.27	−1.62	.51
Kansas	−28.3	1.320	2.98	0.015	0.07	.27
Kentucky	106.23	1.900	4.85	−0.05	0.31	.53
Louisiana	445.54	0.680	0.83	−0.22	−0.62	.00
Maine	−23.26	2.760	2.94	0.01	0.02	.26
Maryland	−401.43	1.510	4.29	0.21	1.29	.48
Massachusetts	−493.09	1.940	3.85	0.25	1.11	.42
Michigan	−311.63	3.740	6.27	0.15	0.58	.66
Minnesota	−166.45	1.890	4.02	0.08	0.40	.43
Mississippi	429.89	2.190	3.72	−0.22	−0.83	.41
Missouri	−146.30	2.160	4.29	0.07	0.32	.46
Montana	83.83	3.250	2.01	0.04	0.06	.09
Nebraska	358.00	0.990	4.02	−0.18	−1.65	.49
Nevada	104.83	2.150	1.77	−0.52	−0.98	.11
New Hampshire	−142.63	1.850	2.02	0.72	1.77	.20
New Jersey	301.02	1.610	4.67	0.15	0.98	.51
New Mexico	792.94	1.070	1.11	−0.40	−0.93	.01
New York	−220.08	1.240	5.02	0.11	0.99	.55
North Carolina	−7.79	1.790	6.86	0.00	0.04	.70
North Dakota	785.24	3.650	2.57	−0.39	−0.62	.22
Ohio	−131.08	2.440	7.82	0.06	0.46	.76
Oklahoma	871.40	0.500	0.80	−0.43	−1.58	.06
Oregon	513.71	3.080	5.74	−0.26	−1.09	.64
Pennsylvania	14.32	1.570	4.69	−0.01	−0.06	.51
Rhode Island	−199.59	1.760	4.03	0.09	0.51	.43
South Carolina	−108.57	2.470	5.82	0.05	0.29	.63
South Dakota	636.88	3.040	4.40	−0.32	−1.05	.50
Tennessee	−13.31	2.000	6.48	0.01	0.00	.68
Texas	410.26	0.410	0.92	−0.21	−1.02	.00
Utah	212.27	2.130	2.61	−0.11	−0.29	.21
Vermont	−455.75	1.660	1.95	0.23	0.61	.09
Virginia	−193.88	1.320	3.83	0.10	0.64	.40
Washington	629.59	2.150	1.78	−0.32	−0.59	.08
West Virginia	−50.42	1.970	4.08	0.02	0.11	.43
Wisconsin	−52.15	1.540	4.50	0.02	0.17	.49
Wyoming	662.74	0.890	0.47	−0.33	−0.40	.00

Note: Data used in analyses are described in Appendix A.
$t \geq |1.72|$ significant at $\alpha = .10$: two-tailed test.
$t \geq |2.07|$ significant at $\alpha = .05$: two-tailed test.
$t \geq |2.82|$ significant at $\alpha = .01$: two-tailed test.

TABLE 9. Value Added by Manufacturing: Classification of States according to
Responsiveness to the National Economy and State-Level
Economic Trends

		Correspondence to National Economic Fluctuations	
		Relatively Independent	Relatively Dependent
State-Level Trend	Growth		AL, CT, FL, GA, IN, ME, MD, MA, MI, MN, MO, MT, NH, NJ, NY, NC, OH, RI, SC, TN, VT, VA, WV, WI
	Decline	DE, IA, LA, NB, OK, TX, WY	AZ, AR, CA, CO, ID, IL, KS, KY, MS, NV, NM, ND, OR, PA, SD, UT, WA

Note: Data used in analyses are described in Appendix A.

The remaining states, all heavily influenced by national-level changes in value added by manufacturing, divide rather neatly into those with positive underlying trends and those with negative underlying trends. Both Michigan and New York fall into the former category while Arizona falls into the latter, but in none of these cases is the trend statistically significant.

Examining change in value added, yet another dimension of state economic performance becomes evident. Like per capita personal income, change in value added by manufacturing is tied to national trends. Indeed, national trends appear to dominate change in value added to a degree much higher than was evident for changes in personal income. Like changes in employment, however, state-level trends in value added by manufacturing were only rarely significant in the statistical sense. This dimension of economic performance would appear to be dominated by business cycles in manufacturing that largely overwhelm state-level patterns.

These results point to several important conclusions about the states and their economies. First, and perhaps most importantly, the states are tightly bound to the performance of the national economy in terms of change in personal income and value added by manufacturing. In essence, the states are not blank slates for policymakers to write upon but are instead moving targets that are being tossed about to varying degrees by national-level economic forces. Second, the states display varying degrees of autonomy from national trends in changes in per capita personal income. Past research has shown that the states most highly dependent on national economic performance also grew most rapidly.[2] While a relatively autonomous state may not benefit as highly from national prosperity, it also would not suffer as much during economic downturns and is in this sense somewhat recession proof. Third, the three economic indicators examined in this analysis were differentially responsive to state and national forces. Changing levels of employment were almost completely divorced from changes at the national level and, for this period at least, the states appear to experience job growth in an almost autonomous fashion. Value added by manufacturing displayed almost the opposite pattern, with most states being influenced dramatically by national-level changes. Per capita personal income fell somewhere between these two extremes.

The state-level trends revealed in this analysis provide at least preliminary evidence that states may be having an impact on their economic performance. Without such a trend it would be hard to argue that state government, policies, or politics were having any appreciable impact on state economies: in a trendless state growth is unpatterned and must be considered to result from forces outside the state. The most unpatterned form of growth occurred in employment and this would suggest strongly that state government, politics, or policy had little impact on job growth over the course of this period. In some states trends were evident in growth in value added by manufacturing, although these trends were quite rare. Therefore, some state governments or policies might be having limited influence on change in this economic indicator. For the most part, this indicator is dominated by the nation's economic fortunes, however. It is in trends in per capita personal income that we find that state-level attributes may be having some influence on economic performance. Almost half the states exhibited statistically significant trends in change in per capita personal income with the effects of national change controlled. These trends, furthermore, differ directionally and substantively. Closer inspection of these trends made clear that things are not always as they seem. Many states with the strongest positive trends were also states typically viewed with disdain for having overly large governments or spending too heavily. Many states suffering decline, however, were found to be those often applauded by proponents of limited government and fiscal restraint. The landscape of state political economy is much clearer from this vantage point.

The Changing Context of State Political Economy

These results make clear that the national context has an enormous effect on most state economies. What is unclear is whether this context is static or dynamic. In other words, is the influence of the national economy on state economies becoming more important (in essence nationalizing the economic performance of the states), or is the national economy becoming less important (with states becoming more fragmented and dissimilar in their economic fortunes) over time? This issue is of obvious importance when considering the economic salience of the contemporary American states. The economic importance of the states may increase or decrease depending on the fragmentation or nationalization of the U.S. economy.

COMPARING STATE AND NATIONAL ECONOMIC EFFECTS

To understand the overall impact of the national economy on the states requires that variation in economic performance be partitioned into that experienced by all states (i.e., national economic performance) and that which was experienced by each state individually (i.e., state economic performance).[3] Pooled cross-sectional time series analysis allows for such a partition. This powerful technique offers special benefits and special problems (see Appendix B). In the current case, a two-way fixed effect model is employed. This model allows intercepts to vary across states and across years. This design is particularly well-suited to the issues of interest in this chapter because it explicitly distinguishes between state and national level variation. By dividing the time series into five-year segments, the changing impact of national and state economies may be examined over time. Using R^2, the model can provide useful estimates of the relative impact of national and state level economic performance over time.

The following model was estimated:

$$Y_{it} = \alpha + \sum_{r=2}^{T} \beta_r X_{rij} + \sum_{r=2}^{N} \delta_r Z_{rij} + e_{it},$$

where

Y_{it} is the annual percentage of change in an economic indicator;

$\displaystyle\sum_{r=2}^{T} \beta_r X_{rij}$ are national (annual) effects captured by indicator variables for each year (minus 1);

$\displaystyle\sum_{r=2}^{N} \delta_r Z_{rij}$ are state effects captured by indicator variables for each state (minus 1); and

e_{it} is the error term.

This model provides estimates of the variation in economic performance experienced generally by all states (i.e., national), and variation experienced uniquely by each state. Comparing the differential impact of state and national effects over time will illustrate the changing character of state economic context.

Beyond the relative impact of national- and state-level forces on state economies, we also may consider the degree of dispersion in state economic performance over time. In this instance, we consider the annual variance in economic indicators for the states. Higher dispersion would suggest that the states were becoming less alike, while lower measures of dispersion would show that the states were becoming more economically homogeneous over time. Taken together, we consider the comparative impact of national and state forces on state economies, and whether states are converging or dispersing in their levels of economic performance.

Per Capita Personal Income. The comparative impact of national and state forces on changes in per capita personal income from 1968 to 1989 is illustrated in Figure 1. While state-level forces were relatively large in the 1968–71 period, they dropped off momentously in 1972–75, and stayed very low through 1983. It could be surmised that the oil crisis of 1973 and the ensuing recessions and stagflation that came to plague the decade came to dominate the economies of almost all states. Beginning in 1984 and continuing through 1989, state variation comes to dwarf national-level influences on state economic performance. Clearly, the 1980s ushered in a changed environment for the states. State variation, rather than national fluctuations, became the dominant source of economic change in the 1980s.

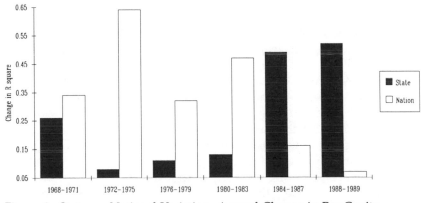

Figure 1. State vs. National Variation: Annual Change in Per Capita
Personal Income, 1968–1989
Source: Computed by author.

Figure 2. Dispersion in Per Capita Personal Income, 1968–1989
Source: Computed by author.

Figure 2 presents the degree of dispersion in per capita personal income over the 1968–89 period. Complementing the results from Figure 1, this figure illustrates a pattern of increasing homogenization among the states up through roughly 1979. Over the course of this early part of the data surveyed, the economy was "nationalizing," with the states becoming increasingly equal in their levels of per capita personal income. After 1980, and especially after 1982, the states exhibit a heightened degree of dispersion in levels of per capita personal income. Increasingly, states became distinct in their levels of per capita personal income during the Reagan era.

The patterns illustrated in Figures 1 and 2 underscore a dramatic change in the economic contexts of states. The impact of the national economy on levels of per capita personal income receded over the course of this period. With the Reagan years, state-level variability in economic performance came to outweigh national-level forces. In this same period, the economy in essence "de-nationalized," with the states becoming much more dispersed in their levels of per capita personal income. In the 1970s, when national-level fluctuations were dominant, and a process of nationalization was taking place in which the states were becoming more equal in levels of per capita income, it is exceedingly unlikely that state-level attributes were exerting any consequential impact on state economic performance. National-level economic forces and processes were dominating patterns of growth in state per capita personal income. However, in the 1980s a new political economic context emerged.

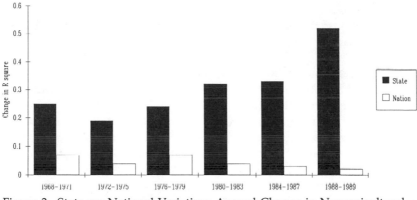

Figure 3. State vs. National Variation: Annual Change in Nonagricultural
Employment, 1968–1989
Source: Computed by author.

Figure 4. Dispersion in Nonagricultural Employment, 1968–1989
Source: Computed by author.

Nonagricultural Employment. A different pattern emerges when nonagricultural employment is considered. As illustrated in Figure 3,
state-level variation has dominated employment change throughout
the period. Figure 4 indicates that the states have become more dispersed in their levels of employment over time. These patterns show
that state factors have served as the predominant forces shaping employment growth, and that employment has grown much more rapidly in some states than in others. The context for employment change

has remained essentially the same throughout the period, with state-level variability dominating the process of change and with states growing apart in their levels of total employment.

Value Added by Manufacturing. Another pattern is illustrated in Figure 5. State and national influence varies substantially over the course of the period. For the most part, national-level fluctuations dominated change in this economic indicator, although state-level forces came to dominate for a brief period in the early 1980s. No stable pattern is evident in the level of dispersion in value added by manufacturing. Figure 6 reveals a cyclical pattern in which states moved toward convergence and then dispersed over the course of the period. While per capita personal income and employment show signs of state-level influence, value added by manufacturing appears to be overwhelmingly influenced by swings in the production cycle that are felt by all states collectively. The cycle of dispersion and fragmentation in this indicator would suggest that growth in manufacturing is, in some periods, concentrated, while in other periods distributed. The normal manufacturing cycle has been observed to disperse technology over time.[4] While manufacturing will be dominated by leading industrial states initially, there is also a diffusion of technology and production processes as producers exploit labor markets and move production closer to markets.

Patterns in States' Economies in the National Context

The states exist in an economic context influenced to varying degrees by the national economy. Manufacturing and especially per capita personal income growth are tied to national economic fortunes in most states while job growth is tied more to state-level factors. Once the pervasive influence of national economic fluctuations is removed, state economic performance appears in a new light. In general, many northern and midwestern states emerge in a much more favorable position when state-level trends, independent of national economic fluctuations, are considered.

Over time, manufacturing growth in the states is dominated by cycles, with state-level influences alternatively increasing and decreasing in importance over time. The dispersion of manufacturing growth also reveals cyclical patterns. Together, these patterns suggest that the expansion or contraction of manufacturing is tied to the vicissitudes of business cycles. Employment growth displayed an almost

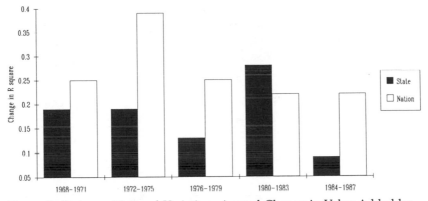

Figure 5. State vs. National Variation: Annual Change in Value Added by
Manufacturing, 1968–1987
Source: Computed by author.

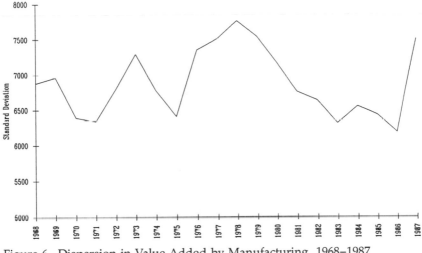

Figure 6. Dispersion in Value Added by Manufacturing, 1968–1987
Source: Computed by author.

opposite pattern: states were a dominant influence on growth in employment throughout the period, with some states growing apart from
others in total employment levels. Patterns of personal income growth
underwent a significant transformation in the wake of policies initiated
in the Reagan era. Growth in income in this period has been tied
more to the states and less to national-level fluctuations. Economically

speaking, states began to grow apart in their levels of per capita personal income in this new era. These patterns indicate that the Reagan era brought about a new economic era for the American states, one where state-level forces have come to play an increasing role in shaping growth in per capita personal income.

Capacity: The Impact of State Government, Party, and Policy on State Economic Performance

Once upon a time, man looked to God to order the world. Then he looked to the market. Now he looks to government. The differences are important.

Anthony King

The preceding chapter made it abundantly clear that the national economy exerts a tremendous influence on the states and their economies. We are left to ask, however, if state government and policy plays any role in shaping the comparative economic performance of states. More specifically, this chapter considers whether the organization and policies of state governments have any tangible economic consequences over time. The analysis proceeds in six steps. First, building from existing literature concerning states and their economies, important features of state government and policy are identified. Second, important alternative influences on state economies are considered. Third, in each instance these important features of state political economy are illustrated by examining the four states from chapters 3 and 4 in detail. Fourth, a general model of state political economy is presented, which incorporates measures of state political capacity, economic development policy, and taxing and spending levels, as well as measures of important alternative influences on state economic performance. Fifth, the model is evaluated empirically using per capita income, employment, and value added by manufacturing, in the pre-Reagan and Reagan eras. Sixth, conclusions about the economic salience of the American states are presented.

State Governments, Policies, and State Economies

The question of whether state governments or their policies have any economic impact involves several auxiliary issues. First, the features of state government and policies that could impinge on state economies must be identified. Second, it is essential to pinpoint which sectors of the economy could be sensitive to governmental influence. Third, it is imperative that alternative forces be incorporated and controlled for in the analysis. Finally, we may ask whether the effects of government and politics are positive, negative, or have no effect at all.

INSTITUTIONAL CAPACITY

According to John Jackson, state governments may influence the health of their economies in many ways. Indeed, he contends the role of state governments in shaping their economies goes beyond the specific economic development policies they adopt. As he notes, "Effective government interventions, in the form of taxing and spending, regulations, and restrictions . . . if done properly, can achieve their stated objectives at the same time that they promote economic growth."[1] Carl Van Horn makes a similar observation. He states that since the governmental reforms of the 1960s that brought heightened professionalism to many state governments, "state government institutions are not only better equipped to assume leadership but also politically motivated to expand the scope of their endeavors."[2] Political institutions with greater capabilities should promote growth over the long run because they are less permeable to organized interests, more effective in policy development and implementation, and provide better management of the public infrastructure.

Virtually every study of the emerging economic activism among the states points to the important role of governors in mobilizing resources to promote economic growth.[3] Alan Rosenthal notes that many governors have taken on new duties, serving as their state's chief sales representative for economic development.[4] While many governors have engaged actively in recent economic development activities, governorships vary considerably in their institutional powers.[5] Stronger governors should be more capable of stimulating economic growth than their weaker counterparts who have fewer appointive, budgetary, or veto powers, and/or limited terms. One observer found that governors with greater formal powers are more inclined to adopt a wide variety of economic development policies.[6]

Dramatic differences in gubernatorial power for Arizona, Texas, Michigan, and New York are illustrated in Figure 7. The governorships

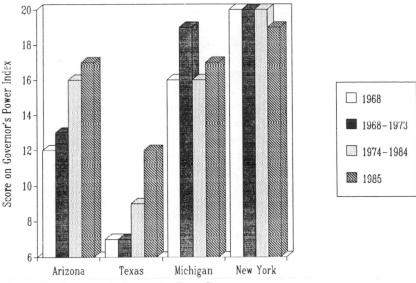

Figure 7. Governor's Power in Four States
   Source: Constructed by author. See Appendix A for sources.

of New York and Michigan are, for the most part, substantially more powerful than those of Arizona and Texas throughout the period, a difference common between Rustbelt and Sunbelt states.

Governors do not make policy in isolation. Their most fundamental power, the veto, is a negative influence on policy. If governors wish to promote programmatic activity to sustain economic growth or otherwise, they must work with the legislature.[7] Legislatures can frustrate programmatic economic development efforts[8] or can serve as a source of policy innovation.[9] A critical variable shaping the legislature's role in the policy process is professionalization. Professionalized legislatures are less influenced by lobbying, particularly that by business.[10] Somewhat surprisingly, business has been found to resist comprehensive economic development plans; it was opposed to the adoption of a comprehensive state industrial policy in Rhode Island.[11] During times of economic stress existing businesses may seek specific protections for their maintenance, but according to Jackson, such maintenance strategies are likely to have small or even negative effects in the long run.[12]

A central dimension of legislative professionalism is the amounts these assemblies spend on their internal operations.[13] Previous studies have identified these budgets to be a key dimension of legislative professionalization.[14] In a recent study by Bowman and Kearny state legislatures were found to have been increasing their capability over the last twenty years and the amounts spent on operating expenditures are a central component of this capability.[15] While ultimately the capability of legislatures rests on many features of their operations, the amounts these bodies spend on their operations can serve as a blunt but plausible and theoretically justified measure of legislative capability. Some states provide their representative assemblies with very meager operating expenditures and are typically characterized as "amateurish;" others provide ample support for staff and services and are typically considered "professionalized." These differences are evident in the four case studies, as can be seen in Figure 8. New York and Michigan provide considerably more resources to their legislators than Texas and Arizona over the course of this period. Complementing the observations of Bowman and Kearny, it can also be seen that each of these states have been increasing these expenditures.

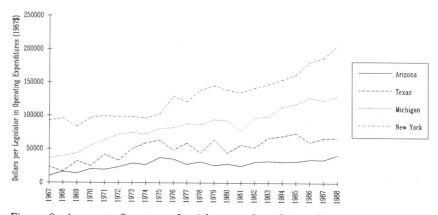

Figure 8. Amounts Spent per Legislator on Legislative Operations in Four
States, 1967–1988
Source: Constructed by author from data in the *Compendium of State
Government Finance,* various years.

Powerful governors and professionalized legislatures are often found together in the states.[16] The correlation of these two measures of government capacity makes evaluation of their independent effects difficult.[17] To evaluate the impact of institutional capacity on growth, the joint influence of governor's power and legislative professionalization are operationalized as a dichotomy. This variable equals one for all states that scored above the national average on each dimension of government capacity in a given year, and zero otherwise.[18]

ECONOMIC DEVELOPMENT POLICIES

There is a notable lack of persuasive evidence indicating that state economic development policies produce beneficial results. Indeed, one can cite a formidable array of studies suggesting that such policies drain state resources and provide little in return.[19] Despite the lack of compelling evidence that these policies work, state leaders have pressed for such policies at an accelerated rate since the recessionary 1970s.[20]

The types of policies and degree of change in their adoption are illustrated in Figures 9–11 for Arizona, Texas, Michigan, and New York. In policies providing tax incentives, financial assistance, and special services for industry, it can be seen that New York and Michigan outraced Arizona and Texas almost universally. This is reflective of a larger regional pattern observed by Peter Eisinger, who noted that "by the baseline year of 1966, northeastern and midwestern states already had in place a greater number of programs than Sunbelt states, even though subsidy programs and tax incentives had originated in the South."[21]

STATE FISCAL POLICIES

Taxation. In many states, political debate is dominated by matters related to taxation and their anticipated effects on a state's business climate. Many policymakers believe that economic growth will be

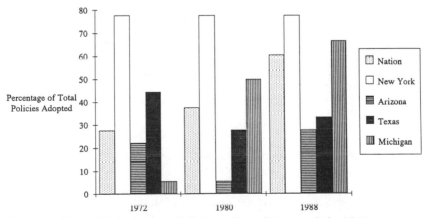

Figure 9. Financial Assistance Policies in Four States and the Nation
Source: Constructed by author with data from *Site Selection Handbook,* various years.

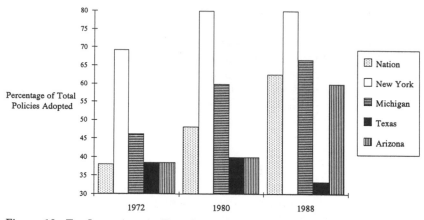

Figure 10. Tax Incentives in Four States and the Nation
Source: Constructed by author with data from *Site Selection Handbook,*
various years.

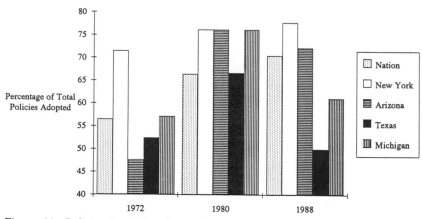

Figure 11. Policies Providing Special Services for Industry in Four States
and the Nation
Source: Constructed by author with data from *Site Selection Handbook,*
various years.

hindered by tax levels that are uncompetitive with other states. While
this notion dominates many debates in state capitols, as noted previously, findings are mixed concerning the economic impact of state
taxation. Nonetheless, the persistent belief that taxes matter warrants
their careful examination.

Figure 12 illustrates the differing levels of per capita taxation in

Arizona, Texas, Michigan, and New York. Somewhat surprisingly, Texas emerges as highest among these four states, bolstered by revenues derived from oil production. Michigan and New York come next and are generally higher than Arizona throughout the period.

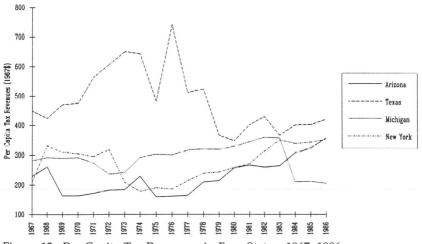

Figure 12. Per Capita Tax Revenues in Four States, 1967–1986
Source: Constructed by author from data in the *Statistical Abstract of the United States*, various years.

Investment Expenditures. Paul Peterson has provided a provocative framework for understanding the policies adopted by cities or states. Peterson believes these governmental units seek to maximize their position vis-a-vis other governments, working within the structural limits provided by the national economy. Peterson divides policies into three categories: developmental, redistributive, and allocational. Developmental policies, of primary interest here, are those that can enhance a state's economic position. Bryan Jones also warns that lumping all expenditures together fails to acknowledge that some policies promote growth while others may retard growth.[22] Attention here centers on what he labels "investment" expenditures. One such investment is the amount spent annually on highways, an infrastructure expenditure that should stimulate state economic growth.[23] Another investment expenditure is that which is spent on education. While Peterson viewed educational expenditures as a redistributive/ allocational hybrid, subsequent research has underscored its importance as a developmental policy.[24] Furthermore, state leaders have been found to view education as a developmental policy.[25] The amounts states invest per capita on highways and education are included in this analysis to explore the stimulative economic effects, if any, of these investment expenditures.

Differences in the rates of these expenditures are illustrated in Figure 13. As can be seen, the rate of these expenditures fluctuates substantially from year to year. New York ranks consistently higher than the other states on these investments in human and physical infrastructure. Texas and Michigan trade second and third places over the course of the period. Texas, fortified with oil revenues, increased these expenditures in the late 1970s and early 1980s but lowered these expenditures in the mid-1980s. Michigan lowered these expenditures during the early 1980s as the state suffered economically during this period, but increased them in the mid-1980s. With only two brief exceptions, Arizona ranked lowest on investment expenditures throughout the period.

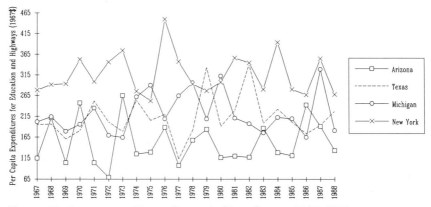

Figure 13. Investment Expenditures in Four States, 1967–1989
        Source: Constructed by author from data in the *Statistical Abstract of the United States,* various years.

POLITICAL PARTIES

Parties have long occupied the attention of students of American state politics. Typically, studies have sought to discern the extent to which parties may affect redistributive policies in the states. The hypothesis stems from V. O. Key's observations on the South over forty years ago. To Key the central issue was, "Who benefits from political disorganization?"[26] An organized and competitive polity, while no panacca, could provide the "institutionalized mechanisms" for the promotion of the interests of the "have-nots." Political disorganization worked to benefit "haves" within a state.[27] Mancur Olson has stimulated interest in the economic impact of political parties. In *Rise and Decline of Nations* he argued that group processes lie at the heart of diminished economic performance.[28] At the same time, however, Olson believed that certain organizations in a state or society could have an economically beneficial impact. The political party is one such organization. He believed that political parties had at least the potential to promote outcomes that would counteract the economically debilitating tendencies of interest groups. Parties, when in control of government, can promote broad-based or "encompassing" outcomes while interest groups pursue narrow, exclusive distributional goals. He thus alerts us to the potential economic impact of party (versus divided) control of state government.

Some students of cross-national political economy have argued that political parties may be economically consequential. On one hand, some have argued that governments of the Left pursue policies that promote the interests of workers, promoting employment and inflation[29] while conservative parties promote policies favorable to the interests of capital.[30] Others have countered that electoral politics lead parties to policy convergence and because they differ so little, they have no effect on economic performance.[31] The hypothesis that is central to this debate about cross-national political economy is that the ideology of political parties controlling government will affect economic performance in democratic nations. In the American states the closest parallel to Left-Right governments is Democratic or Republican control of legislatures and governorships. In the model of state political economy to follow, we consider the economic impact of the type of party controlling government.

Combining Olson's propositions about the economic importance of party government with the observations of some students of cross-national political economy about the economic impact of party ideology leads to the inclusion of Republican and Democratic control variables in the analysis presented shortly. Specifically, Democratic control will identify those states where the Democratic party holds majorities in both the upper and lower chambers of a state's legislature and also controls the state's governorship. Republican control is the precise opposite. Each of these conditions will be compared to states with divided control of their government.

ALTERNATIVE INFLUENCES ON STATE ECONOMIES

To gauge accurately the impact of government and policy on state economic performance requires that alternative economic influences be identified and incorporated into the analysis to rule out spuriousness.

Energy. Probably one of the most momentous economic events of the post–World War II era was brought about by the Arab Oil Embargo in 1973. This incident underscored how important energy was to the American economy. The oil crisis also had the effect of dramatically increasing the value of energy resources in the United States. This change is illustrated in Figure 14 which depicts the per capita value of all mineral resources for the period studied. Clearly, the late 1970s and early 1980s were very good to Texas as the state's oil reserves brought capital to the state. While less pronounced, Arizona also appears to have benefited from mineral resources, at least when compared to Michigan and New York.

In the wake of the oil crisis, and with the heightened value of energy resources, it would seem reasonable to expect these resources to stimulate those states with abundant supplies. In the cross-national context, it has been illustrated how changing markets for oil altered conclusions about political-economic performance of nations.[32] In the United States, it has been found that energy resources stimulated economic growth during the 1970s.[33]

Figure 14. Per Capita Value of Mineral Resources in Four States, 1967–1984
Source: Constructed by author from data in the *Statistical Abstract of the United States,* various years.

To gauge the effects of state-level government and policy on the economic performance of the states, it is imperative that the economic impact of mineral resources is controlled. While certainly oil has played a large role in shaping Texas history and politics, the stimulative economic consequences of oil, particularly those resulting from energy market changes brought about by decisions made in the Middle East, are outside of state control. With a booming market for oil, an energy rich state could grow in spite of, not because of, its governmental practices and public policies. Because of this, it is essential that the stimulative influence of these resources be included as controls in the analysis.

Unionization. Knowledge of the effects of unionization on economic performance is "embryonic."[34] Studies of the economic effects of unions differ concerning their economic consequences. There are economists[35] and political scientists[36] who have argued that unionization retards economic growth. Other schools of economists[37] and political scientists[38] have argued that unionization of the labor force can stimulate economic performance, at least under certain conditions. Because employers may migrate to open-shop states, increasing levels of unionization may be associated with diminished economic growth because of the mobility of capital, not because of the unionized workforce per se.

While the economic consequences of unionization are unclear, it is clear that the states differ markedly in their levels of unionization. This is evident in Figure 15, which illustrates the percentage of unionized workers in the four states. Not surprisingly, the Rustbelt states have much higher labor union membership throughout the period while the Sunbelt states are consistently low. This difference stems from traditions of substantial labor union traditions in New York and Michigan while Texas and Arizona are open-shop states.

Defense Expenditures. In the post–World War II era, defense expenditures have taken on enormous proportions. Past research has found these expenditures to have a significant impact on state economies. For example, research by economists using input-output analysis in the mid-sixties found that southern and western states were the most sensitive to changes in military expenditures.[39] Bruce Russett has argued that the Vietnam war worked to benefit the economies of the South and West. According to Russett, "Under the Johnson administration defense spending became an agent of redistribution of income in favor of the poorer areas in the country, especially the South, and most particularly Texas."[40]

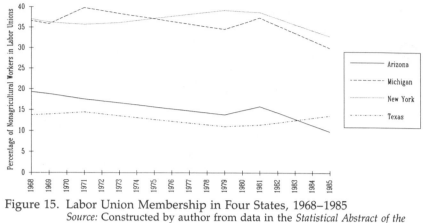

Figure 15. Labor Union Membership in Four States, 1968–1985
Source: Constructed by author from data in the *Statistical Abstract of the United States,* various years.

The high levels of defense expenditures spoken of by Russett are evident in Figure 16. As can be seen, Texas fared very well in defense contracts in the late 1960s and early 1970s when compared to Arizona, Michigan, and New York. However, this disparity leveled off by the mid 1970s. For the remainder of the period studied Arizona, Texas, and Michigan cluster together in levels of per capita defense contracts, while New York remains consistently low throughout the period.

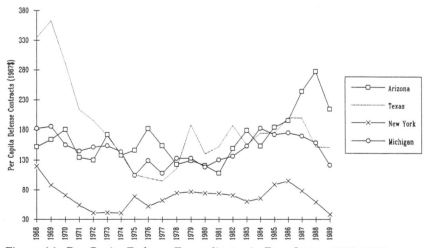

Figure 16. Per Capita Defense Expenditures in Four States, 1968–1989
Source: Constructed by author from data in the *Statistical Abstract of the United States,* various years.

Federal defense allocations have been demonstrated to stimulate state economies.[41] Specifically, per capita defense expenditures in states were associated with heightened growth in per capita personal income, especially during the Reagan years. While state political processes can be imagined to play some role in securing defense contracts, these processes are largely outside the control of state governments. Thus while the economic stimulation associated with these expenditures lends credence to the importance of government policy in motivating economic performance, these policies are determined outside the states. The effects of defense expenditures are thus controlled so as not to distort our picture of the impact of state-level forces on state economies.

Period Effects and the Changing Context of State Political Economy. As we saw in the preceding chapter, the impact of the national economy on state economies has varied considerably since the late 1960s. In the case of per capita income especially, the national economy came to play a much smaller role in the 1980s. There are a number of explanations for this changing context: the globalization of the world economy, increasing competition from abroad, and changing policies at the federal level. A wide variety of literature has underscored the increasing political and economic pressures the states have been placed under in the 1980s. A new era of state-federal relations was ushered in by the Reagan Administration's policies which have altered the functional and economic context of states. On a functional level, as one observer has noted, the signal given by Reagan's devolutionary policies was that the states should do more and they did.[42] On an economic level, another argues that "despite conflicting goals and the constraints of a highly decentralized policy environment, Ronald Reagan has brought about a major redirection in American Economic policy."[43] To gauge the consequences of this changed political and economic environment in the analysis that follows, the economic performance of states will be evaluated before the Reagan policies were implemented (pre-1983) and after the emergence of the New Federalism (1983 and beyond).

A Model of State Political Economy

The research question addressed in this analysis has both a comparative and a longitudinal element: comparative in the sense that the impact of differing levels or features of government and policy on state economic growth is central; longitudinal in the sense that growth is, by definition, a temporal process. This interest in cross-sectional differences and over time change leads to the application of pooled cross-sectional time series analysis (see appendix B). Assessing the economic impact, if any, of state government and policy on the performance of state economies leads to a focus on the manner in which state governmental and policy attributes may alter preexisting patterns of change. Hence, we ask what the effects of state government and policy are, holding economic development and rates of economic performance constant. This interest leads to the incorporation of lagged economic indicators and lagged inertia variables into the analysis. By so doing, the impact of government and policy on growth may be estimated:

$$Y_{it} = \beta_0 + \beta_1 Y_{it-3} + \beta_2(Y_{it-2} - Y_{it-3})$$

$$+ \sum_{k=2}^{k} \gamma_k X_{kit}$$

$$+ \sum_{k=2}^{k} \delta_k Z_{kit}$$

$$+ e_{it},$$

where

Y_{it}	is a state economic indicator;
β_0	is the intercept;
$Y_{it-3} + (Y_{it-2} - Y_{it-3})$	is a lagged dependent variable and a lagged inertia variable;
$\sum_{k=2}^{k} \gamma_k X_{kit}$	are the effects of political capacity, policy and party control described above;
$\sum_{k=2}^{k} \delta_k Z_{kit}$	are the effects of alternative influences also outlined above; and
e_{it}	is the error term.

Evaluation of the Model

To examine the changing role of government and policy in the changing national context, this model will be used to estimate per capita income, nonagricultural employment, and value added by manufacturing from 1968 to 1982, and to estimate the same economic indicators after 1983.

Per Capita Personal Income: 1968–1982. The results of applying the model described above to per capita personal income are presented in Tables 10 and 11 for the years up to and including 1982 and post-1982. Beginning with the pre-1982 results in Table 10, it can be seen that the model is dominated by the lagged variables in the model. Not surprisingly, a state's level of income and rate of change are largely accounted for by preexisting conditions as indicated by the high t-scores for the lagged dependent variable and the inertia variable. The other explanatory variables in the equation are thus left to explain the small increment of change remaining after the preexisting level and rate of change in per capita income are controlled.

TABLE 10. Pooled Analysis of the Growth in Per Capita Personal Income, 1968–1982

Independent Variable	Slope coefficient	Beta	t-Statistic
Government Capacity	20.19	.01	1.57
Economic Development Policy	−1.76	−.02	−2.68**
Investment Expenditures	.07	.10	1.21
Taxation	−.04	−.008	−.94
Democratic Control	8.43	.007	.97
Republican Control	19.17	.01	1.48*
Labor	.68	.01	1.52*
Mineral	.07	.006	.70
Defense	.15	.02	3.01***
Personal Income $(t-3)$	.94	1.02	93.17***
Personal Income Inertia	.78	.28	24.83***
Constant	252.05		6.53***
$R_2 =$	.96		
$N =$	480		
Durbin-Watson $h =$	−.104 (n.s.)		

Note: Data used in analyses are described in Appendix A.
*Significant at $\alpha \leq .10$.
**Significant at $\alpha \leq .05$.
***Significant at $\alpha < .01$.
(n.s.) Not significant ($\alpha \leq .05$).

The variable measuring the effects of institutional capacity emerges as significant at the .1 level and suggests that states with above average legislative professionalism and governor power enjoyed about $20 per year more in per capita personal income in this era. The estimated effects of economic development policy are negative in this period. Supporting the contention in some of the literature that these policies may actually hurt the economic fortunes of a state in the long run, these results suggest that a state's per capita personal income was reduced roughly $1.76 per year for each of these policies in effect, statistically significant at the .01 level. As expected, taxation worked to reduce growth in per capita personal income although this result was not statistically significant. Investment spending was estimated to have a stimulative effect but here too the effects were not statistically significant.

Party control, in general, had a mild stimulative effect on economic performance in this period. It must be remembered that these coefficients are in comparison to divided party control, the excluded category. While both Democratic and Republican control are estimated to exert a positive influence, only Republican control emerges as statistically significant and then only at the .1 level. This associated coefficient suggests that per capita personal income increased roughly $19 in states with Republican control.

Overall, the effects of government, policy, and party on per capita personal income were minimal and mixed in this period. While several of these variables were positively associated with growth, statistically these results were quite tenuous. Statistically speaking, the strongest relationship was a negative one, indicating that state economic development policies harmed growth. Comparatively speaking, the standardized coefficients suggest that investment expenditures had the largest impact on personal income growth, although it should again be noted that this result was not statistically significant. The strong and significant impact of defense expenditures reminds us, however, that governmental spending can have a stimulative effect on state economies.

Of the alternative influences considered, military expenditures are strongly and significantly related to personal income growth in the states in this period. The result concerning this variable indicates that a state's per capita personal income would increase 14 cents in a given year for every dollar per capita received in the preceding year. Clearly, the defense budget has major implications for state economic development. Unionization had a significant positive effect on personal income ($p = .1$) in this period. A 1 percent difference in unionization between the states was associated with a 68 cent difference in per capita personal income annually. While statistically significant, this result is substantively inconsequential. Surprisingly, mineral resources were not significantly related to growth in per capita personal income in this period, although the consequences of this variable emerge as positive, suggesting that personal income in a given year would increase by roughly 7 cents for every dollar of extracted mineral resources in the preceding year, each measured per capita. When analysis is limited to 1973–79, an era in which oil prices escalated rapidly, this variable does have a statistically significant impact on growth in per capita personal income.[44]

Per Capita Personal Income: 1983–1989. A very different picture emerges
when the results of estimating the model in the 1983–89 period are
examined. As before, the preexisting levels of personal income and
rate of change account for the vast majority of variation in personal
income. The effects of government and policy change dramatically in
this era. First, government capacity is positively and significantly
related to growth in per capita personal income. The results indicate
that residents in states with more powerful governors and more highly
professionalized legislatures received over $30 per year more in per
capita personal income annually. Economic development policy now
emerges as significantly and positively related to growth in per capita
income, increasing by almost $4 for every policy a state had in effect.
Taxing and spending also have plausible effects in this period that
are significant at the .05 and .1 level respectively. Each dollar of per
capita taxation reduced personal income by roughly 70 cents. Alternatively, a per capita dollar of investment expenditure was associated
with a 13 cent increase in per capita personal income. The impact of
party control in this era also changes. While neither Democratic nor
Republican control emerges as statistically significant, it is interesting
to note that Democratic party control is positively related to income
growth and Republican party control is inversely related to growth.
While only suggestive, these results concerning party provide additional evidence that activist state government, normally associated
with the Democratic party, helped to stimulate growth in the new
economic context of the 1980s.

The effects of the alternative explanatory variables all emerge as
statistically significant in this period. Mineral resources are inversely
related to change in per capita personal income in this era, which is
not surprising given the drastically altered markets for oil that characterized most of the 1980s. States like Texas and several others that
were resource-dependent suffered during this period, underscoring
the importance of exogenous oil markets to the performance of these
state economies. Military expenditures are again positively and significantly related to growth in per capita personal income. In this new
political economy, the value of a defense dollar increased from 14
cents in the preceding period to 36 cents in this period. The defense
build-up during the Reagan era had dramatic effects on personal
income levels for states receiving large defense contracts.

The coefficient for unionization is positive and statistically significant. In the new economy of the 1980s, labor organization appears
responsible for helping to maintain higher levels of pay. Thus, while
jobs may increase in some states, they may not be well-paying jobs.
In this new economy, government, policy, and unionization work to

TABLE 11. Pooled Analysis of the Growth in Per Capita Personal Income, 1983–1989

Independent Variable	Slope coefficient	Beta	t-Statistic
Government Capacity	31.22	.02	2.21**
Economic Development Policy	3.77	.03	3.08***
Investment Expenditures	.13	.01	1.51*
Taxation	−.07	−.01	−1.77**
Democratic Control	7.52	.05	.59
Republican Control	−7.76	−.03	−.38
Labor	1.60	.02	2.58***
Mineral	−.06	−.05	−5.93***
Defense	.36	.06	5.88***
Personal Income $(t-3)$	1.00	.83	74.09***
Personal Income Inertia	.80	.22	22.49***
Constant	−53.71		−.84
$R_2 =$	.98		
$N =$	334		
Durbin-Watson $h =$	−.10 (n.s.)		

Note: Data used in analyses are described in Appendix A.
*Significant at $\alpha \leq .10$.
**Significant at $\alpha \leq .05$.
***Significant at $\alpha \leq .01$.
(n.s.) Not significant ($\alpha \leq .05$).

maintain higher levels of income for state residents. Of course, the ultimate consequence of this may be to price a state out of the labor market and ultimately stimulate migration of employers elsewhere. As will be noted later, this is the precarious position the states ultimately find themselves in.

Together, it can be seen that the government and policies of the states take on new significance in the 1980s. Using the stadardized coefficients for comparison, it can be seen that preexisting income and growth inertia exert less influence in the 1982 to 1989 period. At the same time, five of the six governmental variables increased in importance. And, as noted, four of the six attained statistical significance in this period. The organization of state government and the policies they adopt affected their rates of growth in personal income in important ways. Recalling Figure 1 in chapter 5, it can be seen that the national economy was in many ways like a rising tide that lifted all boats during the 1960s and 1970s. The dominance of the national economy, for good or ill, basically meant that economic performance varied little according to state political attributes. In the new economy ushered in in the 1980s, state attributes are increasingly important for accounting for change in per capita personal income. States with greater political capacity and more efficient taxation and spending policies were better suited to grow during this period. Rather than hinder growth, government emerges in a positive role in this era.

Nonagricultural Employment: 1968–1982. Although "Jobs, Jobs, Jobs" has been a rallying cry of politicians in both political parties in the last twenty years, this analysis illustrates job growth has not been meaningfully influenced by state governments, policies, or parties. The results of estimating growth in employment are presented in Tables 12 and 13. Examining the coefficient associated with the inertia variable indicates that states with expanding employment were most likely to continue to expand, suggesting that a process of employment dispersion was evident. The dominance of this preexisting growth inertia indicates that forces other than those identified in this model influenced job growth in the 1968–82 period. Government, policy, and party have no statistically discernable impact in this era. The alternative influences in the model, similarly, emerge as statistically inconsequential. Comparing the influences, government capacity and economic policy emerged as the most important influences (beyond inertia and preexisting employment). Yet, given their lack of statistical significance, optimism about government's role in job creation would appear unwarranted. Overall, employment growth was dominated by a preexisting process that is not dislodged or modified by any of the variables in this model.

Nonagricultural Employment: 1983–1989. The picture for employment growth in the 1980s does not change dramatically from the previous

TABLE 12. Pooled Analysis of Growth in Nonagricultural Employment, 1968–1982

Independent Variable	Slope coefficient	Beta	t-Statistic
Government Capacity	3.02	.006	.83
Economic Development Policy	.06	.0003	.04
Investment Expenditures	−.02	−.00001	−.17
Taxation	.02	.0001	.72
Democratic Control	1.42	−.0004	−.58
Republican Control	−3.42	.0006	−1.05
Labor	−.09	−.00005	−.06
Mineral	.02	.0007	.42
Defense	.02	.00009	.16
Nonag. Employment $(t-3)$	1.01	.96	369.47***
Nonag. Employment Inertia	1.02	.24	180.55***
Constant	3.67		.60
$R_2=$	.99		
$N=$	480		
Durbin-Watson $h=$	−1.18 (n.s.)		

Note: Data used in analyses are described in Appendix A.
*Significant at $\alpha \leq .10$.
**Significant at $\alpha \leq .05$.
***Significant at $\alpha \leq .01$.
(n.s.) Not significant ($\alpha \leq .05$).

period. Again, the inertia variable is a dominant influence, suggesting that preexisting patterns of growth are driving change. Of the government, policy, and party variables, only economic development policy emerges as statistically significant ($p = .1$). At best, the result indicates that states with a greater commitment to economic development policies also enjoyed heightened job growth in the new economy of the 1980s. Comparing the standardized coefficients, economic development policies, Republican party control, and labor organization all have comparable impact. Again it must be stressed, however, that this impact was negligible. As in the preceding period, the alternative influences had no statistically discernable influence on job growth in this era.

TABLE 13. Pooled Analysis of Growth in Nonagricultural Employment, 1983–1989

Independent Variable	Slope coefficient	Beta	t-Statistic
Government Capacity	3.03	.0006	.72
Economic Development Policy	.65	.001	1.50*
Investment Expenditures	.01	.0005	.39
Taxation	.02	.0009	.43
Democratic Control	2.28	.0005	.54
Republican Control	8.03	.001	.98
Labor	.27	.001	1.06
Mineral	.09	.0007	1.24
Defense	−.01	.00009	−.84
Nonag. Employment ($t-3$)	1.02	.96	223.94***
Nonag. Employment Inertia	1.01	.14	90.64***
Constant	−26.38		−1.73*
$R_2 =$	.98		
$N =$	334		
Durbin-Watson $h =$	−.75 (n.s.)		

Note: Data used in analyses are described in Appendix A.
*Significant at $\alpha \leq .10$.
**Significant at $\alpha \leq .05$.
***Significant at $\alpha \leq .01$.
(n.s.) Not significant ($\alpha \leq .05$).

While the results concerning the impact of economic development policy lend minor support to the role of activist state government in stimulating state economic performance, the general lack of effects from the other explanatory variables in this analysis underscores the very different nature of employment growth. Job growth may occur for many reasons: proximity to new markets, new technology, or lower production costs. Each of these forces can operate differently. Jobs might grow as a result of technological innovation, such as that in Silicon Valley in California. They may also grow as producers move into locations to take advantage of isolated, lower cost, labor markets. Hence, employment could be stimulated in a politically and economically developed state with substantial commitments to its educational infrastructure. This job growth might be dwarfed by employment gains in a politically and economically less developed state with very low labor costs and proximity to new markets. Furthermore, in the typical production cycle, the technology developed in one state may ultimately be transferred to another state with lower production costs.

The moral from all of this is that employment growth appears largely outside of state governmental control in each period. Jobs grow for different reasons in different places at different times.[45] Ultimately, it is the quality of jobs a state attracts or retains that will shape its economic development. Low labor costs may stimulate employment but would result in low per capita income levels. Economic development is embodied in higher pay and higher employment. As noted above, state action has come to play an important role in stimulating income growth in the new economy. In terms of employment, of the variables considered concerning employment growth, economic development policies emerge as the most important and thus here too state action emerges as important. Together, the effect of state activity in the new economy of the 1980s worked to promote economic development largely by increasing income and, to a much lesser degree, stimulating employment.

Value Added by Manufacturing: 1968–1982. In the 1968–82 period, manufacturing growth was dominated by preexisting inertia, much like employment growth noted above. The only variable to emerge as statistically significant out of those evaluated here was economic development policies. They emerge as inversely related to growth in value added. As noted in the case studies of Michigan and New York, these states, which were among the first to feel the decline of their manufacturing base, were stimulated to adopt a wide array of economic development policies. In this initial period, the states most inclined to adopt these policies may have been suffering the most decline and this would account for the strong inverse relationship. It may have been too early for these policies to have stimulative effects while they were most prevalent in states having the slowest growth in manufacturing.

Value Added by Manufacturing: 1983–1987. Much like the preceding period, neither government, policy, party, nor alternative influences exert a significant influence in growth in manufacturing in the 1983–87 period. Preexisting levels of value added, and especially inertia in

TABLE 14. Pooled Analysis of Growth in Value Added by Manufacturing, 1968–1982

Independent Variable	Slope coefficient	Beta	t-Statistic
Government Capacity	− 68.09	− .004	.93
Economic Development Policy	− 9.04	− .01	− 3.23***
Investment Expenditures	.20	.0002	.99
Taxation	− .14	− .002	− .87
Democratic Control	39.49	.003	1.12
Republican Control	27.88	.001	.51
Labor	1.62	.002	.94
Mineral	.03	.0002	.07
Defense	.17	.002	.77
Value Added $(t-3)$	1.00	1.08	1.97**
Value Added Inertia	.93	.34	90.29***
Constant	144.12		1.67
$R_2 =$	.99		
$N =$	480		
Durbin-Watson $h =$	1.54 (n.s.)		

Note: Data used in analyses are described in Appendix A.
*Significant at $\alpha \leqslant .10$.
**Significant at $\alpha \leqslant .05$.
***Significant at $\alpha \leqslant .01$.
(n.s.) Not significant ($\alpha \leqslant .05$).

value added, were by far the most important determinants of manufacturing growth in this era. States that were growing kept growing and the other influences, governmental and otherwise, did little to disrupt this pattern. One very fundamental difference in this period warrants mention, however. In the later 1980s, pre-existing inertia in value added is no longer a positive determinant of growth in this economic indicator. Instead, inertia was negatively related to manufacturing growth. In this new economy, manufacturing growth was less likely to occur in states that had previously been experiencing growth, and more likely to occur in states where preexisting growth had been low. These results merely confirm what more casual observations would reveal: during the later 1980s many industrially developed states such as Michigan and New York came to experience a degree of resurgence while many previously booming states suffered a degree of stagnation. The results of this analysis indicate, however, that this shift in manufacturing was not directly attributable to government, policy or party, at least as measured here.

Probably the best explanation for the lack of influence of state-level attributes on growth in value added by manufacturing is reflected in Figures 5 and 6 in chapter 5. This economic indicator, it will be recalled, was dominated by national-level forces and was characterized by cycles that no doubt are tied to market contraction and expansion. The national component of variation in this indicator is large in the 1968–82 period, and the 1983–87 period as well. State-level action and other attributes had and continue to have no significant influence on growth in manufacturing as measured here.

TABLE 15. Pooled Analysis of Growth in Value Added by Manufacturing, 1983–1987

Independent Variable	Slope coefficient	Beta	t-Statistic
Government Capacity	− 617.68	− .04	− 1.03
Economic Development Policy	− 5.40	− .004	− .09
Investment Expenditures	− .93	− .01	− .35
Taxation	.48	.009	.25
Democratic Control	547.51	.04	1.04
Republican Control	142.45	.06	.18
Labor	16.15	.02	.76
Mineral	.30	.03	.89
Defense	.44	.07	.20
Value Added $(t-3)$	.71	.73	12.78***
Value Added Inertia	− .31	− .16	− 3.41***
Constant	− 31.53		− 1.73*
$R_2 =$	.48		
$N =$	238		
Durbin-Watson $h =$	.87 (n.s.)		

Note: Data used in analyses are described in Appendix A.
*Significant at $\alpha \leq .10$.
**Significant at $\alpha \leq .05$.
***Significant at $\alpha \leq .01$.
(n.s.) Not significant ($\alpha \leq .05$).

A New American Political Economy?

The evidence presented thus far provides at least partial evidence of significant changes in the role of government in shaping some dimensions of economic performance. Certainly, change in one of the three economic indicators should be related to change in one or both of the others. The stimulative impact of government in one segment of the economy might actually retard growth in another area. Economists commonly note an inverse relationship between per capita income and job growth. In the analysis that follows, interrelationships between these economic variables will be explored. These patterns are illustrated in Figure 17 which presents partial correlation coefficients between economic and governmental/policy variables.[46]

Perhaps the most striking feature of the 1968–82 period is the general lack of relationships between any of the variables. The strongest statistically significant relationships were between economic develop-

State Political Economy: 1968—1982

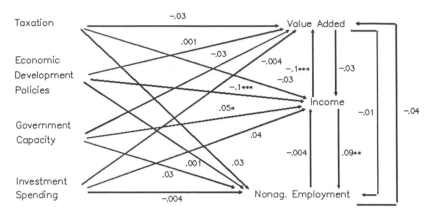

State Political Economy: 1983—1987

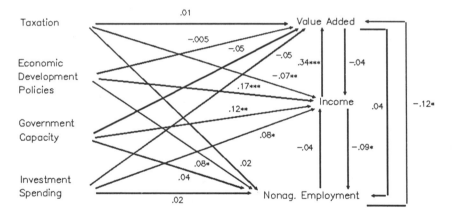

Figure 17. A New American Political Economy?
Source: Computed by author.

ment policy and income, and income and value added by manufacturing. These relationships were negative. This pattern fits well with
what the experiences of states like Michigan and New York were in
this era. They began enacting and implementing many economic development policies in this period yet their manufacturing base eroded
as industry migrated to states with lower incomes. Income growth
worked to stimulate employment growth in this period in a statistically

significant manner ($p = .05$), at least suggesting that labor migrated to locales with higher paying jobs. Overall, the lack of significant influences in this period indicates that growth was determined primarily by preexisting levels of income and inertia.

A notably different pattern emerges in the 1983–87 period. In this era, a number of variables are statistically significant. As noted previously, economic development policies, government capacity, taxation, and investment expenditure all exerted statistically significant influences on growth in per capita personal income. Income growth, in turn, came to exert a strong and significant influence on growth in value added by manufacturing. These findings suggest strongly that the states were having both direct and indirect influences on their standards of living and manufacturing base. State government policies stimulated income growth which stimulated value added by manufacturing. Economic development policies also had a mild, statistically significant influence on employment growth in this period. Income change was inversely related to job growth, as were employment growth and growth in value added by manufacturing. Each of these inverse relationships was significant at only the .1 level, however.

While the relationships presented in Figure 17 must be interpreted cautiously, they nonetheless point quite strongly to fundamental change in the nature of political economy among the American states. First, state government and policy, as noted previously, emerge as significant influences on growth and particularly growth in per capita personal income. Second, income growth was a major influence on growth in manufacturing in this period. These findings complement Eisinger's arguments concerning the entrepreneurial role of the states and the shifting focus on the demand side of the equation.[47] Government has come to matter more and government's role has been to sustain demand by stimulating income growth.

These figures illustrate a fundamental feature of state political economy that is typically missed in the political debates about state economic development. Economic growth is multifaceted. Progress in one area may actually retard growth in another area. In the 1980s the states had an appreciable impact on growth in per capita personal income, an area they appear best suited to affect. Ultimately, however, this income growth was negatively related to job growth. By succeeding in one area, the states may set themselves up to fail in another by pricing themselves out of the labor market. This is the fundamental bind that the states find themselves in.

Patterns in the Impact of State Government, Party, and Policy on State Economic Performance

This analysis allows a more refined view of the economic salience of states. On two of the three economic indicators, state capacity had negligible effects. This was not surprising, given the nature of these indicators revealed in chapter 5. Employment and manufacturing growth have not changed dramatically over the course of the period examined. Throughout the period, employment growth appeared to be characterized by a process of diffusion. Manufacturing growth, alternatively, continued to be dominated by huge cycles in the nation's economy. In both instances, state government capacity was largely incapable of offsetting these powerful and ongoing forces.

Income growth, as indicated in chapter 5, has undergone a fundamental change over the course of the period and it is here that the effects of state capacity emerge. In the wake of policies adopted by the Reagan Administration, state government attributes came to affect growth in per capita personal income, with state capacity having a significant positive influence. The capacity of state governments, the quantity of economic development policies they adopted, and the amounts they spent on developmental policies all were positively related to growth in this new era. Higher levels of taxation, however, served to reduce growth. Throughout the period, party control emerged as largely irrelevant in shaping economic performance. These results indicate that in the more challenging economic environment ushered in by the policies of the Reagan Administration, an era in which states have been placed under greater pressure to do more, state activities matter. In this challenging environment, the institutional characteristics of states, the policies they adopt, and their levels of taxation, all have statistically discernable effects on their rates of growth. In essence, the institutionally more powerful, entrepreneurial state has been better suited to sustain income in the changing economic environment of the 1980s.

These results provide a more coherent picture of the structural limitations that states appear unable to overcome. States cannot overcome larger forces in the national economy such as the diffusion of jobs or the vicissitudes of manufacturing cycles. State capacity also had negligible consequences on income when changes in income were dominated by national economic performance. In essence, states can matter when other more powerful forces are not operating, and they matter in a way that supports an interventionist posture under those conditions. Clearly, however, the benefits of state capacity can be overwhelmed by the re-emergence of national-level forces.

CHAPTER 7

Conclusions: The States and Their Economies in Context

The Puzzle of State Political Economy in a New Light

Normally social scientists turn to theories to solve mysteries. Yet market-oriented and interventionist theories provided incomplete pictures of the process of state economic development. It was when we took into account the conditioning influence of national context that we could understand when and how each of these alternative perspectives could succeed and fail. We can now see that national economic fluctuations dramatically influence state economic performance. Patterns of dependence on the national economy have had differential effects on state economies. This context has undergone significant and important change in the last two decades, particularly in the wake of the Reagan Administration. These findings help us solve some of the puzzles of state economic performance to date: why the energy and efforts to promote growth had few tangible benefits; why formerly booming states declined; and why states in decline experienced economic resurgence.

Close inspection of Arizona, Texas, Michigan, and New York revealed dramatically different development strategies and economic experiences. In Arizona and Texas, probusiness, anti-intervention strategies appeared to succeed, but only as long as national conditions permitted. In states such as these, those in positions to benefit most from growth also had political resources to avoid paying for policies that might sustain the growth. Controlling for the effects of the national economy, the underlying economic trends in these states were less than inspiring. Growth in the developed economies of Michigan and New York paled in comparison to boom states in the South and West. Because the fortunes of many inside and outside of government depended directly or indirectly on governmental programs, these states intervened early to stem the tide of economic decline by employing the institutional resources of the state. Their growth was less tied to the vicissitudes of the national economy and their economies had underlying trends of growth. Dependent, laissez-faire states appear well-suited to grow in periods when the national economy is dominant. Interventionist, programmatic states appear better suited to grow when the nation's economy is not exerting a substantial impact on the states.

Beyond these general observations, six additional findings emanate from this study. First, and most importantly, aspects of state government normally associated with active economic intervention, such as institutional capacity, economic development policy, and investment expenditures, came to exert a positive influence. Second, party control of government by the Democrats or Republicans exerted little appreciable influence on economic growth, despite the often heated and ideological debates between the parties concerning the appropriate path to economic prosperity. This finding corresponds closely to Robert Jackman's argument concerning parties and economic performance in the cross-national setting. He reasoned that party responsiveness to the median voter made it unlikely that they would exert a distinct or appreciable influence on economic performance.[1]

Third, higher per capita taxation was negatively related to growth. This result identifies an important weapon that states are under pressure to use to stimulate growth. Short-run pressures can coalesce to promote tax cuts that can hinder efforts to intervene to promote growth in the long run. States may be lured into a "how low can you go" tax limbo in efforts to compete with their neighbors. Despite its persistence in the states, this approach has obvious limitations. One need only realize that a state with higher taxes may lower them during a downturn while a state with low taxes has nowhere to go with its taxes during bad economic times. Furthermore, research by economists has shown that a dollar of expenditure may stimulate more growth than that lost by a dollar of taxation.[2] In all, states with institutional, policy, taxing, and spending resources appear best suited to cope with challenging economic times.

Fourth, as noted above, the effects of government and policy were primarily limited to income growth, and this limitation has important implications for state economic policymaking. As was seen in the preceding analyses, employment and manufacturing growth were largely outside the reach of state governmental and policy variables. That the effects of government were limited to income growth is, in retrospect, not surprising. Through taxing and spending states directly affect income levels. In addition, by legislation recognizing or restricting collective bargaining, states can indirectly influence wages and salaries. Furthermore, by creating and maintaining institutions of learning and training, the state can prepare workers for higher paying jobs.

State government and policy had minimal effects on employment growth.[3] These findings complement those presented by Richard Feiock. In his analysis of 212 U.S. cities, he found local economic development policies did not affect employment.[4] Often jobs gained in one sector of a state's economy may come at the expense of jobs in another. Also, differing types of employment growth mask changes in a state's economy. Extensive growth in the service sector may not contribute to a state's economic development as greatly as limited growth in manufacturing jobs. In the long run, the quality of jobs a state gains may be more important than the quantity of jobs, yet short-term pressures would seem to favor actions that would emphasize quantity.

Manufacturing growth as measured by value added also showed little sign of responding directly to state political and policy influences. In large measure, manufacturing change appeared to be influenced by large national-level fluctuations. Firms are responsive to many forces and the effects of state-level policies are likely overwhelmed by the dictates of things such as changing markets, consumer tastes, and foreign competition that are no doubt more pressing than the incentives or opportunities afforded by the states.

Fifth, labor organization, typically identified as a bane to growth, was not found to have a notably negative influence on growth. While labor did not have an appreciable impact, positive or negative, on employment or manufacturing growth, unionization was positively related to income growth across the period. Much like the effects of political/governmental variables, collective organization may operate to keep income levels from eroding.

Sixth, defense spending was strongly and significantly related to income growth. Reduced defense expenditures will have a dramatic effect on the economies of states that have had a substantial dependence on defense contracts. At the subnational level, the Cold War defense build up had very tangible but segregated benefits. As Cold War tensions and the defense budget decline, assuming this is indeed the case, many states will find this new era economically challenging.

Context, Capacity, and the Study of State Political Economy

State economic development embodies a wealth of interesting questions. Some of these questions involve the political actors and processes that generate economically relevant outcomes. Other questions concern the economic consequences of government and policy.[5] While the argument and analysis presented in this book cannot answer all of these questions directly they do provide a better footing for addressing them in the future. First, future attempts to evaluate state efforts must take into account the large role of external influences on the open economies of states. Second, evaluation must consider the context created by the national government. Third, evaluation should be realistic about the consequences of state activity: the findings presented here would suggest that state efforts are limited primarily to income.

The results of this study provide peripheral evidence concerning the frameworks that are dominant in economics. None of the empirical results showed the effects of government to be strongly negative in either era. If these indicators can be construed as measuring the presence of government in the economy, however imperfectly, the findings presented here do not support approaches to economic development that stress limited government. To the extent that government did make a difference, its effects were largely positive. This finding would suggest that government intervention can have benefits in certain areas and under appropriate conditions. When state economies were placed under pressure by exogenous economic conditions, government capacity emerged as an important and beneficial influence on economic growth. The laissez-faire approach to economic development appeared to work only when external conditions, believed to be promoted largely by federal intervention, permitted. It is somewhat ironic that national-level liberalism appears to support state-level conservatism. It is equally ironic that national level retrenchment serves to underscore the utility of state-level interventionism.

Too often, arguments concerning the appropriate strategies of state or local governments borrow directly from major economic theories originally targeted at nations. These arguments thus treat states as if they were autonomous economic entities. Close inspection of the actual interplay of political and economic forces at the subnational level reveals dimensions that neither the neoclassical nor interventionist models adequately consider. These theories are highly general in character and are usually applied as blanket diagnoses or prescriptions. As Paul Peterson has argued, however, local governments exist in a dramatically different context than nation-states.[6]

Applying economic theories developed for nations to the states is fraught with peril. The result has been misinterpretation and debate. Perhaps the best example of treating states as if they were nations is Mancur Olson's provocative but controversial *Rise and Decline of Nations*.[7] The argument he develops in that book is largely about nations, as the title implies. His thesis, described earlier in this volume, is that group processes undermine the economic vitality of nations as political processes come to displace market efficiencies. While generally focusing on nations, Olson nonetheless turns to the American states for empirical support for his argument. He finds that the older a state is, the slower its economy had been growing from the 1940s through the 1970s—results that support his thesis about the long-term ossification that attended group processes in a society.

Others have sought to empirically evaluate Olson's thesis but the results have contributed to debate[8] focusing on the power of groups and their effects on state economies, which often treated states implicitly like nations. The debate continues because findings concerning the effects of state-level influences from these studies vary from important to irrelevant or largely symbolic. The results presented here may place these alternative interpretations in a more coherent setting. The effects of states on their economies are not fixed but variable due to the openness of state economies. The impact of exogenous forces can distort our evaluations of state-level effects on state economies. Also, probably too great an emphasis has been placed on the economic impact of groups and too little on the economic importance of public institutions and policies. A comprehensive evaluation of the effects of political processes on state economies must consider the fluctuating context of states and variations in their political capacity as well as the patterns of influence and their effects at the state level.

The Limits of State Economic Development

Peterson argues that the contexts of subgovernments place limits on their ability to enact policies, with redistribution a more appropriate role for the national government and development more appropriate for cities or states. He observes that "the interests of local government require that it emphasize the economic productivity of the community for which it is responsible. Because they are open systems, local governments are particularly sensitive to external changes. To maintain their local economic health, they must maintain a local efficiency that leaves little scope for egalitarian concerns. These limits on local governments . . . require that these governments concentrate on developmental as against redistributive objectives."[9] Central (i.e., national) government may better focus on redistributive goals, according to Peterson, at least partly because of the availability of powers to curb the impact of the external world environment on the nation's economy.[10]

States may not be as well-suited to promote development as Peterson's argument suggests. Lateral competition could render states ineffectual in promoting development goals. If states are forced to abandon taxation to sustain short-term growth, they will be unable to promote adequately development through expenditures. Furthermore, the empirical results reported here reveal that the positive economic impact of state government was limited to personal income and the conventional economic wisdom suggests that high income and job growth are inversely related. Thus, when the states do succeed in stimulating income growth, they may also retard job growth. When this occurs, short-term pressures typically mount to attract or retain employers, often with tax cuts. Ultimately, states may all adopt "beggar thy neighbor" strategies, with public education and technical and physical infrastructure suffering. States would ultimately lose many of the resources necessary to sustain their economies and growth would be of the dependent, not self-sufficient, variety. The important lesson to be drawn from this is that, for the states, economic development is multifaceted, embodying many conflicting political and economic forces. Unfortunately, many state efforts have failed to take this into account.

When external forces are stimulating growth, there is little state governments can do to influence positively this exogenous growth. At best they might remove impediments and seek to attract this growth. States with lower cost labor, aesthetic or natural resources, and lower taxes may be better suited to pursue external sources of growth. Hence, within the United States, over time, there have been recurring cycles as these less economically and politically developed states have experienced "catch-up" gains. Just as nature abhors a vacuum, the American economy appears to abhor large disparities in income for extended periods. No matter how vibrant the northeastern or midwestern economy became during the 1980s, at some point the vacant offices, lower labor costs, and more favorable tax climate of states such as Texas emerged as a lure.

Portions of the country that lag economically almost inevitably will experience a surge in their economies simply because of cost advantages in those states. While such growth is to be expected, it is hardly something that state policymakers can rely on. Indeed, all too often this form of catch-up growth is taken as a sign that minimal government is the final solution to their economic perils. Unfortunately, the inevitable course seems to be that as growth comes to these states, their cost advantages diminish; eventually, growth diminishes and these states lose their short-term advantages.

The next cycle is easy to anticipate. If all states were equal in terms of their cost and tax advantages, and the value of their natural resources, it is only through technological innovation and the level of skills in the workforce that growth can occur. It is at this juncture that the political capacity of the state can matter. States with well-developed institutions of higher learning stimulate technological innovation and produce a better educated workforce. These same states have the capacity to invest in infrastructure that can create a more productive environment for producers. Together, of course, these come at the cost of higher taxes. So here too we can anticipate an inevitable cycle. The spillover effects of technology are great. Education and ideas financed in one state may be easily transferred to another. This is especially likely when cost advantages in other states come to serve as a magnet. Unfortunately, the costs of this technology and education are borne almost strictly by the state providing it. In the long run, the mobility of labor and capital to lower tax states places very severe limits on the economic capacity of activist states. The result is analogous to the prisoner's dilemma mentioned in chapter 1: states need technological innovation to grow, but competition between them produces an outcome that falls far short of optimal. Tiebout argued that the mobility of capital and labor could produce efficiency in the provision of public goods.[11] Yet investment expenditures may impose short-run costs with only a promise of long-run benefits. People may vote with their feet before those benefits can be secured. Sensitivity to short-run costs and the mobility of capital and labor makes it difficult for states to make beneficial long-term investments.

In the long run, nations, states, and firms with deep pockets to invest in research and technology may be best situated to grow. States more constrained by the mobility of producers and workers to keep taxes low will be least capable of capitalizing on an increasingly important form of growth. In the end, given the highly permeable and open nature of their economies, all states are very constrained in the amounts they may tax. Consequently it is improbable that the states can serve as the engine for innovation that may be essential for their sustained economic growth, let alone for the growth of the whole nation. Thus, lateral competition between states, typically viewed as an efficiency inducing force on state governments, also may render them incapable of making the types of investments necessary to compete in an increasingly complex and technologically sophisticated global marketplace. As noted in one popular account, "Simply cutting the budget deficit and raising private investment is not enough to enable America to regain its competitive edge. . . . Unless the nation finds ways to boost public investment significantly, . . . America's future may be at risk."[12]

The states cannot act like nations. They cannot control who lives within their boundaries nor who leaves. If a firm moves outside the state, the state cannot retaliate by imposing tariffs that protect firms making the same products within the state. This openness makes states very sensitive to forces outside their control. State efforts thus take place in a volatile environment. Concerted economic development efforts appear to have benefits, however. States with government capacity, economic development policies, and higher levels of investment expenditure appear better suited to sustain income growth as the United States political economy changes and as the global economy becomes more challenging.

If the effects of economic development efforts at the state level were obvious, there would be no mystery of state political economy nor would debates continue among economists about the appropriate course of action. After extensive evaluation of the states and their economies, it would be especially gratifying if the findings could point unequivocally to the appropriate course of action for policymakers. Unfortunately, the effects of policy on economic performance are subtle and any recommendation must be cautious. Hopefully, however, the findings presented in this book can provide some insight into the limits of action at the state level, and the challenges inherent in pursuing action.

A New American Political Economy

Several observers of the American states and their economies have suggested that there may be a new, emergent political economy in America. The new entrepreneurial state represents a small-scale version of a "mixed economy" in which state government has undertaken an expanded, if still modest, role in the economic realm. The results presented here show that the economic context and role of the American states have undergone a significant transformation over the last two decades. At this point, however, there are several reasons to question the sufficiency and durability of state efforts in the economic realm.

First, as noted above, with the changing global economy and the retreat of the national government in many policy areas, the economies of the American states now appear to be caught in boom and bust cycles. If, as argued here, state-level efforts can serve as engines of growth under limited circumstances, this success can place these states at a comparative disadvantage to states with less ambitious (and costly) economic development plans. New York or Michigan may create conditions ripe for innovation and growth, but technology and production practices developed at least partly under the auspices of these states can be transferred to Texas or Arizona.

While state politicians may benefit little from extensive economic development programs, they may suffer if taxes in their state are high and a national recession drags their economy down. As the 1980s closed, a national recession placed politicians and economic development programs in many states in jeopardy. In the midst of this economic slump, Michigan turned James Blanchard out of office and replaced him with a governor much less inclined to use the public sector to stimulate the state's economy. This new governor initially called for elimination of the state's economic development programs but later settled for a scaled-down program.[13] The sluggishness of the nation's economy was placing pressure on politicians in many states, particularly those with ambitious taxing/spending programs, as political leaders in these states fought to stave off budget deficits. All this underscores the fragility of state economic development efforts. Like a house of cards, they may be assembled with great care, yet, with a single jolt, come tumbling down.

Second, past research indicates that state politicians are not notably rewarded or punished for their management of state economies. As one scholar notes, "If there is little evidence that state politicians are blamed or rewarded according to their performance as economic managers, there is reason to question how substantially those politicians are guided by the belief they will be."[14] He adds that if conditions in a state differ from those in neighboring states, voters hold the governor only minimally responsible.[15] That voters do not expect too much from their governors is probably good because as Samuel Peltzman observes, "As chief executive in a small open economy without a central bank, the governor cannot conduct very powerful macro policy."[16] Hence, the public's expectations and the government's economic capabilities are quite limited. Given the conditions of low public expectations, minimal political incentives, and comparatively limited economic policy capacity, it is hard to imagine that the states can emerge as dominant agents of economic growth in the United States. The nature of the national economy could shape the degree of economic accountability of state politicians, however. John Chubb found that state politicians were largely isolated from accountability for the performance of their economies. His study covered the 1940 to 1982 period, however, an era he notes was characterized by an increasingly homogenous national economy.[17] Under those conditions it would not be surprising that state politicians were not being held accountable for their state's economic performance. Studies employing more recent data, however, reveal that this process of homogenization subsided in the 1980s.[18] As the reach of the national economy recedes, and the reach of the global economy expands, new economic influences may be descending upon the states, placing their politicians under increasing pressure.

The unfortunate feature of the emergent economic accountability at the state level is that it runs almost exclusively in one direction. Given the limited policy leverage in their economies and the restricted and seldom acknowledged benefits from intervention, the incentives for state politicians should lead them to the "tax cut limbo." In the open economies of the states, even courageous leadership is unlikely to offset the structural impediments to sustained, aggressive state intervention.

In the early years of the republic, capital was scarce and the new nation faced very formidable competition from Europe. Shortages of both labor and capital created an environment that was ripe for technological innovation even in the early part of the nineteenth century. In this setting, state governments promoted economic development by providing legal and financial inducements to encourage certain activities. Rapid growth and innovation were the result.

In the wake of World War II, while facing military competition from the Soviet Union, the United States faced little economic competition and could dominate the world's markets. At the end of the twentieth century, the United States is once more confronting a shortage of capital and faces stiff challenges from Japan and Europe both at home and abroad. In this context, the states have again emerged to promote legal and financial inducements to stimulate economic development and the findings reported here show that features of the entrepreneurial state have been associated with growth. Yet, as outlined above, there are many structural impediments to sustained and aggressive state-level intervention and in the newly emergent technologically sophisticated global economy, aggressive intervention may be more crucial then ever.

In the new economy, there may be increasing rather than decreasing returns from investment. For example, although high-tech products like semiconductors and computers require large investments, per unit production costs fall with rising output that stimulates demand, lowering prices further and stimulating still more demand. Unlike commodities, where demand is finite, demand for knowledge-based technologies may continually expand. Those with the deepest pockets may be most able to get a head start and this can be vitally important in the new competition. The states have been active in trying to stimulate innovation and investment to promote economic growth but, as noted above, these efforts are very fragile. Thus, while the comparative analysis of government intervention presented here indicates that government can make a difference, there are still many reasons to question the sufficiency of state-level efforts for sustaining national economic competitiveness.

Data and Measurement

States

It has become conventional in studies of state economic performance to exclude Hawaii and Alaska.[1] This study follows this convention and is limited to the forty-eight contiguous states.

Dependent Variables

There are many ways in which state economic performance could be evaluated. The central concern of this inquiry is with the rate at which a state develops economically. In a developed economy citizens can enjoy more material rewards and a per capita measure of income growth would appear suitable.[2] Per capita income also captures the distribution of growth.[3] Alternatively, some economists have advocated the use of indicators of productive capacity to measure economic growth.[4] As noted by Usher, there is no clear-cut right or wrong choice.[5] Consequently, three separate indicators of economic performance are examined:

Income 1968–1989: per capita personal income in constant (1967) dollars. Source: *Survey of Current Business*, various years.

Nonagricultural Employment, 1968–1989. Source: *Survey of Current Business*, various years.

Value Added by Manufacturing, 1968–1987. Source: *Survey of Current Business*, various years.

Explanatory Variables

The logic underlying the inclusion of these variables is presented in chapter 6.

POLITICAL ATTRIBUTES

Political Capacity. Equals one, if in a given year a state is concurrently above the national average in governor's power and legislative capability; equals zero otherwise.

Governor's Power. Schlesinger Index of formal governors' powers has been computed for various years, providing longitudinal measurement of the power of governors. Listed below are the years the indices were used in the current time series and the years from which they were computed.

   1968–69: Schlesinger Index, computed from 1960 data.[6]

   1970–71: Schlesinger Index, computed from 1969 data.[7]

   1972–81: Schlesinger Index, computed from 1971 data.[8]

   1982–85: Schlesinger Index, computed from 1982 data.[9]

Legislative Capability. Amounts spent on internal control by legislatures (per legislator) in constant (1967) dollars, lagged one year, computed by author. Sources: control budgets taken from U.S. Bureau of the Census, *Compendium of State Government Finance*, various years; number of legislators obtained from *Book of the States*, various years.

Policy. Total number of tax incentives, financial assistance, and state support for industry policies in states. Source: *Site Selection Handbook*, various years.

Investment Expenditure. Total per capita state expenditure for education and highways in constant (1967) dollars, lagged one year. Source: computed from data in the *Statistical Abstract of the United States*, various years.

Taxation. Total annual per capita taxes in constant (1967) dollars, lagged one year. Source: computed from data in the *Statistical Abstract of the United States*, various years.

Republican and Democratic Party Control. These respective variables equal one in states where the Republican (or Democratic) parties control both houses of the legislature and the governorship simultaneously and equal zero otherwise.

ALTERNATIVE INFLUENCES

Energy. Annual per capita mineral revenues, lagged one year. Source: computed from data in the *Statistical Abstract of the United States,* various years.

Unionization. Annual percentage of nonagricultural employees that are members of labor unions, lagged one year. Source: computed from data in the *Statistical Abstract of the United States,* various years.

Defense. Annual per capita receipts of military contracts in constant dollars, lagged one year. Source: computed from data in the *Statistical Abstract of the United States,* various years.

Methodology

Ordinary Least Squares

Ordinary least squares regression (OLS) was employed in the state-by-state analyses presented in chapter 5. Examination of Durbin-Watson's h indicated that autocorrelation was not present in any of the models. This is probably due to the inclusion of the trend (i.e., year) variable in each.

Least Squares with Dummy Variables

To evaluate the relative impact of national- and state-level forces on state economies in chapter 5, least squares with dummy variables was used. Stimson provides an excellent discussion of this technique.[1] This technique incorporates unit (i.e., state) and time (i.e., year) dummy variables to capture cross-sectional and temporal variation. While this technique suffers when degrees of freedom are an issue, it is excellent for illustrating national- and state-level variation since degrees of freedom are not an issue in this case. The state dummy variables capture variation unique to each state while the year dummy variables capture change in all states in a given year(s) and thus can be said to reflect national economic performance. This approach has been applied in studies of state policy and political economy.[2]

GLS-ARMA

For the analyses in chapter 6 diagnostics were run to assess the extent to which problems with heteroskedasticity and autocorrelation were evident. Examining residuals derived from OLS analyses, the autocorrelation functions (ACF) and partial autocorrelation functions (PACF) indicated that first-order autocorrelation was present in several of the analyses. In addition, analyses of residual variance indicated that the residuals were not constant across cross-sections. To rectify these problems, the GLS-ARMA procedure developed by Kmenta[3] was employed. This procedure estimates and specifies time-dependent processes in residuals and incorporates a weighted least squares weighting procedure to deal with heteroscedasticity, eliminating the need for temporal and unit dummy variables and the lost degrees of freedom they entail. Because the models include a lagged dependent variable, Durbin-Watson's h is presented in the tables as a test for autocorrelation. The statistic is distributed as a standard normal variable. The null hypothesis (i.e., no autocorrelation) was not rejected for any of these models.

NOTES

PREFACE

1. Mancur Olson, *The Rise and Decline of Nations* (New Haven: Yale University Press, 1982).

2. Paul Brace, "The Political Economy of Collective Action," *Polity* 20 (Summer 1988): 648–64.

3. Paul Brace, "Isolating the Economies of States," *American Politics Quarterly* 17 (August 1989): 256–76; Brace, "The Changing Context of State Political Economy," *Journal of Politics* 53 (May 1991): 297–317.

4. Paul Brace and Youssef Cohen, "How Much Do Interest Groups Influence Economic Growth?" *American Political Science Review* 83 (December): 1297–1308; Brace and Robert Dudley, "Military Expenditures and State Economic Growth," in *Public Policy and Economic Institutions*, ed. Mel Dubnick and Alan Gitelson (Greenwood, Conn.: JAI Press, 1991); Brace and Gary Mucciaroni, "The American States and the Shifting Locus of Positive Economic Intervention," *Policy Studies Review* 10, no. 1 (1991): 151–72.

CHAPTER 1. THE MYSTERY OF STATE POLITICAL ECONOMY

1. "U.S. State Lawmakers: Growth Management Top Priority," *Site Selection* (April 1991): 256; Richard L. Holman, "Embattled State Governments Give Entrepreneurship Another Boost," *Wall Street Journal*, March 14, 1991.

2. See Ronald C. Fisher, *State and Local Public Finance* (Glenview, Ill.: Scott, Foresman, 1988).

3. Albert O. Hirschman, *Shifting Involvements: Private Interest and Public Action* (Princeton: Princeton University Press, 1982).

4. Richard P. Nathan, "The Role of the American States in American Federalism," in *The State of the States*, ed. Carl E. Van Horn (Washington, D.C.: Congressional Quarterly Press, 1989), 17.

5. Ibid., 18.

6. Advisory Commission on Intergovernmental Relations, *The Question of State Government Capability* (Washington, D.C.: Advisory Commission on Intergovernmental Relations, January 1985).

7. See Cletus C. Coughlin and Thomas B. Mandelbaum, "Have Federal Spending and Taxation Contributed to the Divergence of State Per Capita Incomes in the 1980s?" *Federal Reserve Bank of St. Louis Review* 71 (July/August 1989): 29–42; and Cadwell L. Ray and R. Lynn Ritenoure, "Recent Regional Growth Patterns: More Inequality," *Economic Development Quarterly* (August 1987): 240–48.

8. David Osborne, *Laboratories of Democracy* (Cambridge: Harvard Business School Press, 1988), 249.

9. Ibid., 249.

10. David Lampe, *The Massachusetts Miracle* (Cambridge: MIT Press, 1988), 113.

11. Adam Smith, *An Enquiry into the Nature and Causes of The Wealth of Nations* (Edinburgh: Adam and Charles Black, 1776).

12. See Michael Bleany, *The Rise and Fall of Keynesian Economics* (New York: St. Martin's, 1985).

13. F. Hayek, *The Road to Serfdom* (Chicago: University of Chicago Press, 1944); Hayek, *The Constitution of Liberty* (Chicago: University of Chicago Press, 1960); and Hayek, *Rules and Order* (Chicago: University of Chicago Press, 1973).

14. F. Hayek, *Capitalism and Freedom* (Chicago: University of Chicago Press, 1962).

15. Milton Friedman and Rose Friedman, *Free to Choose* (New York: Harcourt Brace Jovanovich, 1980).

16. D. Colander, ed., *Neo-Classical Political Economy* (Cambridge: Ballinger, 1984).

17. See, e.g., James M. Buchanan, *The Limits of Liberty: Between Anarchy and Leviathan* (Chicago: University of Chicago Press, 1975); Buchanan and Gordon Tullock, *The Calculus of Consent* (Ann Arbor: University of Michigan Press, 1962); Buchanan and Richard E. Wagner, *Democracy in Deficit* (New York: Academic Press, 1977); William A. Niskanen, *Bureaucracy and Representative Government* (Chicago: Aldine-Altherton, 1971).

18. Mancur Olson, *The Logic of Collective Action* (Cambridge, Mass.: Harvard University Press, 1965).

19. Stephen Newman, *Liberalism at Wits' End* (Ithaca, N.Y.: Cornell University Press, 1984), 158.

20. T. N. Srinivasan, "Neoclassical Political Economy, the State and Economic Development," *Asian Economic Review* 3, no. 2 (1985): 38–58 at 40.

21. Karl Polanyi, *The Great Transformation* (Boston: Beacon Press, 1957), 140–41.

22. Geoff Hodgson, *The Democratic Economy* (Harmondsworth: Penguin Books, 1984), 78.

23. James W. Dean, "Polyarchy and Economic Growth," in *The Political Economy of Growth*, ed. Dennis C. Mueller (New Haven: Yale University Press, 1983).

24. Paul Brace, "The Political Economy of Collective Action: The Case of the American States," *Polity* 20 (Summer 1988): 648–64.

25. John Maynard Keynes, *The General Theory of Employment, Interest, and Money* (London: Macmillan, 1936).

26. Buchanan and Wagner, *Democracy in Deficit.*

27. Goran Therborn, "West on the Dole," *Marxism Today* 29, no. 6 (1985): 6–10; Therborn, *Why Some People Are More Unemployed Than Others* (London: Verso, 1986).

28. See Bleany, *Rise and Fall of Keynesian Economics,* 153.

29. Charles Lindblom, *Politics and Markets: The World's Political and Economic Systems* (New York: Basic Books, 1977).

30. See Dean, "Polyarchy and Economic Growth."

31. Bryan Jones, Lynn W. Bachelor, with Carter Wilson, *The Sustaining Hand: Community Leadership and Corporate Power* (Lawrence: University of Kansas Press, 1986), 15.

32. John H. Mollenkopf, *The Contested City* (Princeton: Princeton University Press, 1983).

33. Paul Peterson, *City Limits* (Chicago: University of Chicago Press, 1981).

34. C. M. Tiebout, "A Pure Theory of Local Expenditures," *Journal of Political Economy* 64 (1956): 416–24.

35. Timothy Bartik, *Who Benefits from State and Local Economic Development Policies?* (Kalamazoo, Mich.: W. E. Upjohn Institute for Employment Research, 1991).

36. Robert Axelrod, *The Evolution of Cooperation* (New York: Basic, 1984).

37. Fisher, *State and Local Public Finance,* 83–84.

38. For example, using the unweighted ideology scores computed by Wright, Erikson, and McIver, Texas, Arizona, Michigan, and New York rank 9, 10, 34, and 41 respectively among the states in their degree of ideological conservatism. Gerald Wright, Robert Erikson, and John McIver, "Measuring State Partisanship and Ideology with Survey Data," *Journal of Politics* 47 (1985): 469–89.

39. Using the weighted party identification scores computed by Wright, Erikson, and McIver (ibid.), Texas, Arizona, Michigan, and New York rank 11, 24, 31, and 37 among the states in the degree of their identification with the Democratic party.

40. Using the General Policy Liberalism Index computed by David Klingman and William W. Lammers ("The 'General Policy Liberalism' factor in American State Politics," *American Journal of Political Science* 28 [1984]: 598–610), Texas, Arizona, Michigan, and New York rank 30, 45, 10, and 1 respectively among the states in their policy liberalism.

CHAPTER 2. NATIONAL CONTEXT AND STATE CAPACITY

1. Albert O. Hirschman, *Shifting Involvements: Private Interest and Public Action* (Princeton: Princeton University Press, 1982).

2. See, e.g., Mancur Olson, "The South Will Fall Again: The South as Leader and Laggard in Economic Growth," *Southern Economic Journal* 50 (April 1983):

917–32; Walter W. Rostow, "Regional Change and the Fifth Kondratief Up-swing," in *The Rise of the Sunbelt Cities*, ed. David C. Perry and Alfred J. Watkins, *Urban Affairs Annual Reviews*, vol. 14 (Beverly Hills: Sage, 1977); Douglas E. Booth, "Long Waves and Uneven Regional Economic Growth," *Southern Economic Journal* 53 (October 1986): 448–60.

3. Stephen Skowronek, *Building a New American State* (Cambridge: Cambridge University Press, 1982), 20.

4. Ibid., 23.

5. Jacob E. Cooke, ed., *The Reports of Alexander Hamilton* (New York: Harper, 1966), 166.

6. Gallatin called for federal intervention in the construction of roads and canals to "shorten distances, facilitate commercial and personal intercourse, and unite the most remote quarters of the United States." In his estimation, "no other single operation, within the power of Government, can more effectually . . . strengthen . . . that Union." Quoted in Leonard D. White, *The Jeffersonians: A Study of Administrative History, 1801–1829* (New York: Macmillan, 1951), 474–75.

7. Arthur M. Schlesinger, Jr., *The Cycles of American History* (Boston: Houghton Mifflin, 1986), 228.

8. Carolyn Webber and Aaron Wildavsky, *A History of Taxation and Expenditure in the Western World* (New York: Simon and Schuster, 1986), 379.

9. Ibid., 381.

10. Lewis H. Kimmel, *Federal Budget and Fiscal Policy, 1789–1958* (Washington, D.C.: Brookings Institution, 1959), 57.

11. Jonathan R. T. Hughes, *The Governmental Habit: Economic Controls from Colonial Times to the Present* (New York: Basic Books, 1977), 238.

12. William Letwin, ed., *A Documentary History of American Economic Policy Since 1789* (New York: W. W. Norton, 1972).

13. Gerald D. Nash, *State Government and Economic Development: A History of Administrative Policies in California, 1849–1933* (Berkeley: University of California, 1964), 19.

14. See E. A. Johnson, *American Economic Thought in the Seventeenth Century* (London, 1923); and Hughes.

15. Louis Hartz, *Economic and Democratic Thought: Pennsylvania, 1776–1860* (Cambridge: Harvard University Press, 1948).

16. This term is from Carter Goodrich, "The Revulsion Against Internal Improvements," *Journal of Economic History* 10 (November 1950): 145–69.

17. L. Ray Gunn, "The Crisis of Distributive Politics: The Debate Over State Debts and Development Policy in New York, 1837–1842," in *New York and the Rise of American Capitalism*, ed. William Pencak and Conrad Edick Wright (New York: New York Historical Society, 1989), 195.

18. Richard F. Fenno, Jr., *The Power of the Purse: Appropriations Politics in Congress* (Boston: Little, Brown, 1966), 43–44.

19. Schlesinger, Jr., *Cycles of American History*, 234.

20. See, e.g., *Lochner v. New York*, 198 U.S. 45 (1905); *Adkins v. Children's Hospital*, 261 U.S. 525 (1923).

21. See *Munn v. Illinois*, 94 U.S. 113 (1876).

22. *Wabash, St. Louis and Pacific Railroad Co. v. Illinois*, 118 U.S. 557 (1886).

23. *Chicago, Milwaukee and Saint Paul Railroad Co. v. Minnesota*, 132 U.S. 418 (1890).

24. Skowronek, *Building a New American State*, 160.

25. Schlesinger, Jr., *Cycles of American History*, 234.

26. Skowronek, *Building a New American State*, 135.

27. James Bryce, *The American Commonwealth*, vol. 2 (New York: Putnam, 1959), 651.

28. See Theodore Roosevelt, *Message to Congress*, December 8, 1908.

29. Wilson noted that "Without the watchful . . . interference of the government, there can be no fair play between individuals and such powerful institutions as the trusts." Woodrow Wilson, *The New Freedom* (Englewood Cliffs, N.J.: Prentice Hall, 1961), 164.

30. Webber and Wildavsky, *History of Taxation and Expenditure*, 456.

31. Ibid.

32. Carl E. Van Horn, "The Quiet Revolution," in *The State of the States*, ed. Carl E. Van Horn (Washington, D.C.: Congressional Quarterly Press, 1989), 4.

33. James C. Cobb, *The Selling of the South* (Baton Rouge: Louisiana State University Press, 1982).

34. Bruce A. Williams, "Regulation and Economic Development," in *Politics in the American States: A Comparative Analysis*, ed. Virginia Gray, Herbert Jacobs, and Robert B. Albritton (Glenview, Ill.: Scott, Foresman, 1990), 483.

35. Alan K. Campbell, "State and Local Taxes, Expenditures, and Economic Development," in *State and Local Taxes on Business*, ed. Charles F. Conlan (Princeton: Tax Institute of America, 1965), 195–208.

36. R. Stryk, "An Analysis of Tax Structure, Public Service Levels, and Regional Economic Growth," *Journal of Regional Science* 7 (Winter 1967): 175–84.

37. Lynn Browne, "Regional Investment Patterns," *New England Economic Review* (July/August 1980): 5–23.

38. Thomas Plaut and Joseph Pluta, "Business Climate, Taxes and Expenditures, and State Industrial Growth in the United States," *Southern Economic Journal* 50 (September 1983): 99–119.

39. Richard K. Vedder, "Rich States, Poor States: How High Taxes Inhibit Growth," *Journal of Contemporary Studies* (Fall 1982): 19–32.

40. W. Warren McHone, "State Industrial Development Incentives and Employment Growth in Multistate SMSAs," *Growth and Change* 15 (October 1984): 8–15.

41. Roger Schmenner, *Making Business Location Decisions* (Englewood Cliffs, N.J.: Prentice-Hall, 1982).

42. Timothy Bartik, "Business Location Decisions in the United States: Estimates of the Effects of Unionization, Taxes, and Other Characteristics of States," *Journal of Business and Economic Statistics* 3 (January 1985): 14–22.

43. Herzik's results cited by Beyle in Gray, Jacobs and Albritton, *Politics in the American States*, 232.

44. Peter Eisinger, *The Rise of the Entrepreneurial State* (Madison: University of Wisconsin Press, 1988).

45. R. Scott Fosler, ed., *The New Economic Role of American States* (New York: Oxford University Press, 1988), 3.

46. See, for example, David Osborne, *Laboratories of Democracy* (Boston: Harvard Business School Press, 1988); David Lampe, ed., *The Massachusetts Miracle* (Cambridge: MIT Press, 1988).

47. Eisinger, *Rise of the Entrepreneurial State*, 10.

48. Fosler, *New Economic Role*.

49. Ibid., 4.

50. See, e.g., Eisinger, *Entrepreneurial State*; Fosler, *New Economic Role*; Osborne, *Laboratories of Democracy*.

51. Eisinger, *Entrepreneurial State*, 9.

52. Robert Premus, et al., *The U.S. Climate for Entrepreneurship and Innovation*, a report prepared for the Joint Economic Committee, U.S. Congress (Washington, D.C.: Government Printing Office, 1985), ix.

53. Fosler, *New Economic Role*, 312.

54. Eisinger, *Entrepreneurial State*, chap. 6.

55. Ibid., 338.

56. Fosler, *New Economic Role*, 328.

CHAPTER 3. THE POLITICAL ECONOMY OF DEPENDENCE IN ARIZONA AND TEXAS

Epigraphs: Quoted in Peter Wiley and Robert Gottlieb, *Empires in the Sun: The Rise of the New American West* (New York: G. P. Putnam, 1981), 171; and Robert Suro, "Three States, Once Fat on Oil, Try to Break with Past," *New York Times*, January 14, 1990.

1. Bruce Mason, "Arizona: Interest Groups in a Changing State," in *Interest Groups in the West*, ed. Ronald J. Hrebenar and Clive Thomas (Salt Lake City: University of Utah Press, 1987).

2. Ibid., 25.

3. Wiley and Gottlieb, *Empires in the Sun*, 166.

4. Mason, "Arizona," 24.

5. Ibid., 25.

6. Ibid.

7. 1980 Census.

8. Sarah McCally Morehouse, *State Politics, Parties, and Policy* (New York: Holt, Rinehart and Winston, 1981).

9. David Osborne, *Laboratories of Democracy* (Boston: Harvard Business School Press, 1988).

10. Mason, "Arizona," 26.

11. Ibid., 27.

12. The Citizen's Conference on State Legislatures, *The Sometimes Governments: A Critical Study of the 50 State Legislatures* (New York: Bantam, 1971).

13. Larry Landry, "Arizona," in *The New Economic Role of American States*, ed. R. Scott Fosler (New York: Oxford University Press, 1988), 267.

14. Ibid., 259.

15. Lee R. McPheters, "Arizona's Economic Outlook," in *The Southwest Economy in the 1990s: A Different Decade*, ed. Gerald P. O'Driscoll, Jr., and Stephen P. A. Brown (Boston: Kluwer Academic Publishers, 1989).

16. *Christian Science Monitor*, March 21, 1989.

17. "Arizona's Boom Fades to a Mirage as Several Sectors Hit a Severe Slump," *Wall Street Journal*, May 9, 1989.

18. *Barron's* citation taken from Bruce Sankey, "Bashing Phoenix: Are the Good Times Really Over?" *Arizona Republic*, December 25, 1988.

19. "Arizona's Boom Fades."

20. Sankey, "Bashing Phoenix."

21. "Funds Down, Bellies Up: Bankruptcy Filings Hit Record Number," *Mesa Tribune*, January 5, 1992.

22. "Job Cuts, Bankruptcies Top Reports for 1991," *Mesa Tribune*, December 29, 1991.

23. "Symington Sued in S and L Loss: Accused of Negligence with 11 Other Ex-Southwest Officials," *Arizona Republic*, December 17, 1991.

24. Poll conducted by Behavior Research Center, Phoenix, Arizona, January 11–14, 1992.

25. "39% Want Governor to Quit," poll reported in *Mesa Tribune*, January 6, 1992.

26. "Symington: Cut Taxes," *Mesa Tribune*, January 14, 1992.

27. Ibid.

28. Quoted in "Training for Jobs: Highest Priority," *Arizona Republic*, January 12, 1992.

29. V. O. Key, Jr., *Southern Politics* (New York: Vintage Books, 1949).

30. See James C. Cobb, *The Selling of the South* (Baton Rouge: Louisiana State University Press, 1982); Gavin C. Wright, *Old South, New South: Revolutions in the Southern Economy Since the Civil War* (New York: Basic Books, 1986).

31. Jared E. Hazleton, "Natural Resources in Texas," in *Dynamics of Growth: An Economic Profile of Texas*, ed. Louis J. Rodriguez (Austin, Tex.: Madrona Press, 1978).

32. Stanley A. Arbingast and Dennis Richardson, "Military Payrolls and the Texas Economy," *Texas Business Review*, 41 (March 1967).

33. Computed from data in *Statistical Abstract of the United States* (Washington, D.C.: U.S. Government Printing Office, 1958, 1964, 1972).

34. Suro, "Three States."

35. Peter Applebome, "The Good Old Boys Confront Some Harsh New Realities," *New York Times*, September 21, 1986.

36. Cobb, *Selling of the South*, 151.

37. Applebome, "The Good Old Boys," quoting historian Joe B. Frantz.

38. Keith Mueller, "Explaining Variation and Change in Gubernatorial Powers, 1960–1982," *Western Political Quarterly* 38 (1985): 424–31; Joseph Schlesinger, "The Politics of the Executive," in *Politics in the American States*, ed. Herbert Jacobs and Kenneth N. Vines (Boston: Little, Brown, 1965; 2d ed. 1971).

39. Morehouse, *State Politics*, 215.

40. Suro, "Three States."

41. Ibid.

42. Peter Applebome, "Economic Boom in the South Ebbs as Advantages Diminish," *New York Times*, July 1, 1989.

43. Tom R. Rex, "Arizona Lags Behind on Economic Development," *Arizona Business* 38 (February 1991): 1.

44. Mark Ivey, "Crisis in the Gulf Eases Crisis in the Oil Patch," *Business Week*, no. 3176 (September 24, 1990).

CHAPTER 4. THE POLITICAL ECONOMY OF INTERVENTION IN MICHIGAN AND NEW YORK

Epigraphs: The Path to Prosperity: The Findings and Recommendations of the Task Force for a Long Term Economic Strategy for Michigan (East Lansing: State of Michigan, 1984), 70; and Omnibus Economic Development Act of 1987, Laws of New York, Chapter 839, State of New York.

1. John E. Jackson, "Michigan," in *The New Economic Role of American States*, ed. R. Scott Fosler (New York: Oxford University Press, 1988).

2. Virginia Gray, Herbert Jacobs, and Kenneth Vines, eds., *Politics in the American States*, 4th ed. (Boston: Little, Brown, 1982).

3. Ibid., 318.

4. *The Path to Prosperity*, 1.

5. Harry Anderson, with Jacob Young, "Escape to the Sun Belt," *Newsweek*, April 27, 1981: 67–68.

6. Reported in Wallace W. Bierman, "The Validity of Business Climate Rankings: A Test," *Industrial Development* 153 (March/April 1984): 17–25.

7. Peter K. Eisinger, *The Rise of the Entrepreneurial State* (Madison: University of Wisconsin Press, 1988) 134.

8. New York ranked 48 in the Fantus survey, and between 39 and 46 in the three Grant surveys.

9. In a recent evaluation of these rankings, Charles L. Skoro finds that some are *inversely* related to economic growth. He argues that these rankings should be seen for what they are—political statements that have little verifiable economic content. Skoro, "Rankings of State Business Climates: An Evaluation of Their Usefulness in Forecasting." *Economic Development Quarterly* 2 (May 1988): 138–52.

10. Fosler, *New Economic Role*, 120.

11. *The Path to Prosperity*, vi.

12. Reported in Fosler, *New Economic Role*, 121.

13. "What New York Can Learn from Texas," *Society*, May/June 1976, 48–50.

14. Harry N. Schribner, "Federalism and the American Economic Order," *Law and Society Review* 10 (1975): 57–100.

15. Nathan Miller, *The Enterprise of a Free People: Aspects of Economic Development of New York State During the Canal Period, 1792–1838* (Ithaca: N.Y.: Cornell University Press, 1962).

16. This statute was passed in 1817.

17. L. Ray Gunn, "The Crisis of Distributive Politics: The Debate Over State Debts and Development Policy in New York, 1837–1842," in *New York and the Rise of American Capitalism: Economic Development and the Social and Political History of an American State, 1780–1870*, ed. William Pencak and Conrad Edick Wright (New York: New York Historical Society, 1989).

18. Frank J. Mauro and Glenn Yago, "State Government and Targeting in Economic Development: The New York Experience," *Publius* 19 (Spring 1989): 63–82, at p. 68.

19. Morton Schoolman and Alvin Magid, eds., *Reindustrializing New York State: Strategies, Implications, Challenges* (Albany: SUNY Press, 1986), 36.

20. Ibid.

21. "Targets of Economic Opportunity: A Strategy for Economic Development in New York State" (Albany: Executive Chamber, State of New York, 1979).

22. Omnibus Economic Development Act of 1987, 1608.

23. Neal R. Peirce, "Sunbelt's Future: Lessons from Up North?" *National Journal* 18 (February 15, 1986): 409.

24. Ibid. See also Bernard L. Weinstein and Harold T. Gross, "The Rise and Fall of the Sun, Rust, and Frost Belts," *Economic Development Quarterly* 2, no. 1 (1988): 9–18.

25. Peirce, "Sunbelt's Future," 409.

CHAPTER 5. CONTEXT: ISOLATING THE ECONOMIES OF STATES

Epigraph: "Presidential Race Beckons Arkansas Governor," *New York Times*, May 29, 1987.

1. It is interesting to note that these states ranked among the most rapidly growing in Olson's evaluation of state economic performance. See Mancur Olson, *The Rise and Decline of Nations* (New Haven: Yale University Press, 1982).

2. Paul Brace, "Isolating the Economies of States," *American Politics Quarterly* 17 (August 1989): 256–276, at p. 270.

3. This approach was developed in Brace, ibid.

4. See *The Path to Prosperity: The Findings and Recommendations of the Task Force for a Long Term Economic Strategy for Michigan* (East Lansing: State of Michigan, 1984).

CHAPTER 6. CAPACITY: THE IMPACT OF STATE GOVERNMENT, PARTY, AND POLICY ON STATE ECONOMIC PERFORMANCE

Epigraph: Anthony King, "Overload: Problems of Governing in the 1970s," *Political Studies* 23 (1975): 162–74, at p. 166.

1. John E. Jackson, "Michigan," in *The New Economic Role of American States*, ed. R. Scott Fosler (New York: Oxford University Press, 1988), 101.

2. Carl E. Van Horn, "The Entrepreneurial State," in *The State of the States*, ed. Van Horn (Washington, D.C.: Congressional Quarterly Press, 1989), 209.

3. See, e.g., Susan B. Hansen, "Targeting in Economic Development: Comparative State Perspectives," *Publius* 19 (Spring 1989): 47–62, at p. 57; David Osborne, *Laboratories of Democracy* (Boston: Harvard Business School Press, 1988); Charles R. Warren, "Indiana," in Fosler; Jackson, "Michigan," in Fosler; Timothy J. Bartik, "Tennessee," in Fosler op cit; Douglas C. Henton and Steven A. Waldhorn, "California," in Fosler; Larry Landry, "Arizona," in Fosler; Dennis C. Grady, "Governors and Economic Development Policy: The Perception and the Reality of Their Influence," *Policy Studies Journal* 17, no. 4 (1989): 879–94.

4. Alan Rosenthal, "The Newest Role for Governors: Entrepreneur," in *State Government 1988–1989*, ed. Thad Beyle (Washington, D.C.: Congressional Quarterly Press, 1990).

5. For differences in the institutional powers of governors between states and over time see Sarah McCally Morehouse, *State Politics, Parties, and Policy* (New York: Holt, Rinehart and Winston, 1981); Keith Mueller, "Explaining Variation and Change in Gubernatorial Powers, 1960–1982," *Western Political Quarterly* 38 (1985): 424–31; Joseph Schlesinger, "The Politics of the Executive," in *Politics in the American States*, ed. Herbert Jacobs and Kenneth N. Vines (Boston: Little, Brown, 1965; 2d ed. 1971).

6. Margery M. Ambrosius, "The Role of Occupational Interests in State Economic Development Policy-Making," *Western Political Quarterly* 42 (March 1989): 53–68.

7. Sabato makes this point. Larry Sabato, *Goodbye to Goodtime Charlie*, 2d ed. (Washington: Congressional Quarterly Press, 1983).

8. Osborne makes this observation in *Laboratories of Democracy*.

9. See Henton and Waldhorn, "California," for a discussion of the positive role played by a state legislature.

10. L. Harmon Zeigler, "Interest Groups in the States," in *Politics in the American States*, ed. Virginia Gray, Herbert Jacobs, and Kenneth Vines, 4th ed. (Boston: Little, Brown, 1983).

11. Mark S. Hyde, William E. Hudson, and John J. Carroll, "Business and State Economic Development," *Western Political Quarterly* 41 (March 1988): 181–91.

12. Jackson, "Michigan."

13. John Grumm ("The Effects of Legislative Structure on Legislative Performance," in *State and Urban Politics: Readings in Comparative Public Policy*, ed. Richard Hofferbert and Ira Sharkansky [Boston: Little, Brown, 1971]) and Morehouse (*State Politics*) find this as central at two points in time. See also Paul Brace and Daniel Ward, "The Institutionalization of the American Statehouse: 1968–1985," paper presented at the annual meeting of the Midwest Political Science Association, Chicago, April 1989.

14. Grumm, "Effects"; Morehouse, *State Politics*.

15. Ann O'M. Bowman and Richard C. Kearny, "Dimensions of State Government Capability," *Western Political Quarterly* 41 (June 1988): 341–62.

16. In the 1968 to 1989 period the bivariate correlation between legislative resources and governor's power was .599.

17. In methodological terms this is a problem with multicollinearity, a condition where one or more of the explanatory variables are highly correlated. In essence, this is a problem of the limits of the data. Too few instances of weak governors and strong legislatures, and the converse, are present and thus it becomes impractical to make an independent judgment about each institution. In a past study of state political economy including data up to 1985, no serious problems with multicollinearity were encountered. See Paul Brace, "The Changing Context of State Political Economy," *Journal of Politics* 53 (May 1991): 297–317. In the extended data analyzed here, multicollinearity was evident and this affected the efficiency of the coefficients estimated for each variable.

18. This variable captures the impact of joint legislative and gubernatorial institutional capacity and avoids problems with multicollinearity.

19. See, e.g., Susan B. Hansen, "The Effects of Economic Policies on Economic Growth," paper presented at the annual meeting of the American Political Science Association, Washington, D.C., September 1984; Michael Kieschnick, "Taxes and Growth: Business Incentives and Economic Development," in *State Taxation Policy*, ed. Michael Barker (Durham, N.C.: Duke University Press, 1983); Thomas Plaut and Joseph Pluta, "Business Climate, Taxes and Expenditures, and State Industrial Growth in the United States," *Southern Economic Journal* 50 (September 1983): 99–119; R. J. Vaughn, *State Taxation and Economic Development* (Washington, D.C.: Council of State Planning Agencies, 1979).

20. Ambrosius, "Role of Occupational Interests"; Peter K. Eisinger, *The Rise of the Entrepreneurial State* (Madison: University of Wisconsin Press, 1988).

21. Eisinger, ibid., 62.

22. Paul Peterson, *City Limits* (Chicago: University of Chicago Press, 1981); see also Bryan Jones and Arnold Vedlitz, "Higher Education Policies and Economic Growth in the American States," *Economic Development Quarterly*, 2, no. 1 (1988): 78–87.

23. Thomas R. Dye, "Taxing, Spending and Economic Growth in the American States," *Journal of Politics*, 42 (1980): 1085–1107.

24. Brace, "Changing Context"; Bryan Jones, "Public Policies and Economic Growth in the American States," *Journal of Politics* 52 (February 1990): 219–33; Jones and Vedlitz, "Higher Education Policies"; Michael Wasylenko and Therese McGuire, "Jobs and Taxes: The Effects of Business Climate on States' Employment Growth Rates," *National Tax Journal* 38 (December 1985): 497–511; Hwang Sung-Don and Virginia Gray, "External Limits and Internal Determinants of State Public Policy," *Western Political Quarterly* 44, no. 2 (1991): 277–98.

25. Thomas Dye, *American Federalism: Competition among Governments* (Lexington, Mass.: Lexington Books, 1990).

26. V. O. Key, *Southern Politics* (New York: Vintage Books, 1949), 307.

27. Ibid., 307–10.

28. Mancur Olson, *The Rise and Decline of Nations* (New Haven: Yale University Press, 1982).

29. See Douglas Hibbs, "Political Parties and Macroeconomic Policies," *American Political Science Review* 71 (1977): 1467–87. But see Geoffrey Garrett and Peter Lange, "Performance in a Hostile World: Domestic and International Determinants of Economic Growth in the Advanced Capitalist Democracies," *World Politics* 38 (1986): 517–45; Lange and Garrett, "The Politics of Growth: Strategic Interaction and Economic Performance in Advanced Industrial Democracies, 1974–1980," *Journal of Politics* 47 (1985): 792–827; and "The Politics of Growth Reconsidered," *Journal of Politics* 49 (1987): 257–74.

30. See David Cameron, "The Expansion of the Political Economy," *American Political Science Review* 72 (1978): 1242–61; and "Social Democracy, Corporatism, Labour Quiescence, and the Representation of Economic Interests in Advanced Capitalist Society," in *Order and Conflict in Contemporary Capitalism*, ed. J. Goldthorpe (New York: Oxford University Press, 1984); F. Castles, *The Impact of Parties* (Beverly Hills: Sage, 1982); Garrett and Lange, "Performance"; Alexander Hicks and Duane Swank, "On the Political Economy of Welfare Expansion," *Comparative Political Studies* 17 (1984): 81–118; Lange and Garrett, "Politics" and "Politics Reconsidered"; M. Schmidt, "The Role of Parties in Shaping Macroeconomic Policy," in Castles, *Impact of Parties*; and "The Welfare State and the Economy in Periods of Economic Crisis," *European Journal of Political Research* 11 (1983): 1–26.

31. See Robert W. Jackman, "The Politics of Economic Growth in Industrial Democracies, 1974–80: Leftist Strength or Northsea Oil?" *Journal of Politics* 9 (1987): 242–56; and "The Politics of Economic Growth Once Again," *Journal of Politics* 51 (1989): 646–61; Richard Rose, *Do Parties Make A Difference?* 2d ed. (London: Chatham House, 1984).

32. Jackman, "Politics of Economic Growth in Industrial Democracies."

33. Brace, "Changing Context."

34. Barry T. Hirsch and John T. Addison, *The Economic Analysis of Unions: New Approaches and Evidence* (Boston: Allen & Unwin, 1986), 293.

35. E.g., Timothy Bartik, "Business Location Decisions in the United States: Estimates of the Effects of Unionization, Taxes and Other Characteristics of States," *Journal of Business and Economic Statistics* 3 (January 1985): 14–22; Albert Rees, "The Effects of Unions on Resource Allocation," *Journal of Law and Economics*, 6 (October 1963): 69–78; Ronald S. Warren, Jr., "The Effect of Unionization on Labor Productivity: Some Time Series Evidence," *Journal of Labor Research* 6 (Spring 1985): 199–207.

36. Dye, *American Federalism*.

37. E.g., Charles Brown and James Medoff, "Trade Unions in the Production Process," *Journal of Political Economy* 86 (June 1978): 355–78.

38. E.g., Garrett and Lange, "Performances"; Lange and Garrett, "Politics," and "Politics Reconsidered"; Paul F. Whitely, "The Political Economy of Economic Growth," *European Journal of Political Research* 11 (1983): 197–213.

39. Wasily Leontif et al., "The Economic Impact—Industrial and Regional—of an Arms Cut," *The Review of Economics and Statistics* 47 (1965): 217–41.

40. Bruce Russett, *What Price Vigilance?* (New Haven: Yale University Press, 1970), 69.

41. Brace, "Changing Context"; Brace and Gary Mucciaroni, "The Amer-

ican States and the Shifting Locus of Positive Economic Intervention," in *American Politics, Public Policy, and Liberalism's Future*, ed. Mucciaroni, *Policy Studies Review*, 10 (Spring 1991): 151–72; Brace and Robert Dudley, "Military Expenditures and State Economic Growth," in *Public Policy and Economic Institutions*, ed. Mel Dubnick and Alan Gitelson (Greenwood, Conn.: JAI Press, 1991).

42. Richard P. Nathan, "The Role of the States in American Federalism," in *State of the States*, Van Horn, 29.

43. Henry C. Kenski, "The Politics of Economic Policymaking: The Shift from Carter to Reagan," in Marianne C. Clarke, *Revitalizing State Economies* (Washington, D.C.: National Governors' Association, 1986), 77.

44. See Brace, "Changing Context"; Brace and Mucciaroni, "American States."

45. This point is made in *The Path to Prosperity: The Findings and Recommendations of the Task Force for a Long Term Economic Strategy for Michigan* (East Lansing: State of Michigan, 1984).

46. The paths presented in Figure 17 show the partial correlations between the variables of central interest, controlling for the alternative influences identified above and preexisting levels and inertia in each economic indicator. Republican and Democratic party control was included in analysis but these paths were not illustrated for presentational clarity.

The path diagrams provide an indication of the impact of government on each economic indicator, the impact of each economic indicator on the other, controlling for preexisting wealth and inertia, as well as the impact of mineral wealth, defense expenditures, labor organization, party control, and national trends.

Partial correlations between government/policy variables and economic indicators were taken from the models presented in Tables 10–15. The intercorrelations between economic indicators were calculated by estimating each economic indicator as a function of its preceding year's level, and the rate of change in it and the other economic indicators.

47. Eisinger, *Entreprenerial State*.

CHAPTER 7. CONCLUSIONS: THE STATES AND THEIR
ECONOMIES IN CONTEXT

1. Robert W. Jackman, "The Politics of Economic Growth in Industrial Democracies, 1974–80: Leftist Strength or Northsea Oil?" *Journal of Politics* 49 (1987): 242–56.

2. See Michael Wasylenko and Therese McGuire, "Jobs and Taxes: The Effects of Business Climate on States' Employment Growth Rates," *National Tax Journal* 38 (December 1985): 497–511; L. Jay Helms, "The Effects of State and Local Taxes on Economic Growth: A Time Series-Cross Section Approach," *Review of Economics and Statistics* 67 (November 1985): 574–82; Leslie Papke, "Subnational Taxation and Capital Mobility: Estimates of Tax-Price Elasticities," *National Tax Journal* 40 (June 1985): 191–204.

3. Peter K. Eisinger, *The Rise of the Entrepreneurial State* (Madison: University

of Wisconsin Press, 1988); *The Path to Prosperity: The Findings and Recommendations of the Task Force for a Long Term Economic Strategy for Michigan* (East Lansing: State of Michigan, 1984).

4. Richard C. Feiock, "The Effects of Economic Development on Local Economic Growth," *American Journal of Political Science* 35 (August 1991): 643–45.

5. Eisinger has noted in *The Rise of the Entrepreneurial State* that there are many issues involved in evaluating the economic consequences of state activities: for example, do economic policies elicit investments that otherwise would not have occurred; do economic development policies create new employment, or do they merely shift jobs from one locale to another; is economic development mainly an exercise in symbolic politics for the purpose of enhancing a state's business climate reputation?

6. Paul Peterson, *City Limits* (Chicago: University of Chicago Press, 1981).

7. Mancur Olson, *The Rise and Decline of Nations* (New Haven: Yale University Press, 1982).

8. Kwang Choi, A Study of Comparative Rates of Economic Growth, Ph.D. diss., University of Maryland, 1979; Mancur Olson, "The Political Economy of Comparative Growth Rates," in *The Political Economy of Growth*, ed. Dennis C. Mueller (New Haven: Yale University Press, 1983); Frederick L. Pryor. "A Quasi-test of Olson's Hypothesis," in Mueller, *Political Economy*; Thomas R. Dye, "Taxing, Spending and Economic Growth in the American States," *Journal of Politics* 42 (1980): 1085–1107; Margery M. Ambrosius, "Olson's Thesis and Economic Growth in the American States: The Role of Interest Group Strength in State Economic Development Policymaking, 1969–1980," paper presented at the meeting of the Midwest Political Science Association, Chicago, 1985; and "The Role of Occupational Interests in State Economic Development Policy-Making," *Western Political Quarterly* 42 (March 1989): 53–68; Paul Brace, "The Effects of Organized Interests on State Legislatures," paper presented at the annual meeting of the American Political Science Association, New Orleans, August 1985; "Markets, Institutions, and Political Participation: Policy Access and Economic Growth among the American States," paper presented at the annual meeting of the Western Political Science Association, Eugene, Oregon, 1986; "The Political Economy of Collective Action: Effects of Political Development upon Rates of Economic Growth in the States, 1965–1980," paper presented at the annual meeting of the American Political Science Association, Washington, D.C., 1986; "Legislatures and Economic Performance," paper presented at the annual meeting of the American Political Science Association, Washington, D.C., 1988; "The Political Economy of Collective Action," *Polity* 20 (Summer 1988): 648–64; Brace and Phillip Baumann, "Markets versus Polity: The Politics of State Economic Growth," paper presented at the annual meeting of the Midwest Political Science Association, Chicago, 1986; Brace and Youssef Cohen, "How Much Do Interest Groups Influence Economic Growth? *American Political Science Review* 83 (December 1989): 1297–1308; Brace and Robert Dudley, "National Determinants of the Rise and Decline of States," paper presented at the annual meeting of the Midwest Political Science Association, Chicago, 1985; Virginia Gray and David Lowery, "Interest

Group Politics and Economic Growth in the U.S. States," *American Political Science Review* 82 (March 1988): 109–31; Allan Brierly and Richard Feiock, "The Political Economy of State Economy Growth: A Production Function Approach," paper presented at the annual meeting of the Midwest Political Science Association, Chicago, 1988.

9. Peterson, *City Limits*, 69–70.

10. Ibid.

11. C. M. Tiebout, "A Pure Theory of Local Expenditures," *Journal of Political Economy* 64 (1956): 416–24.

12. Gene Koretz, "Economic Trends," *Business Week*, no. 3118 (August 7, 1989): 18.

13. From conversation of author with economic development personnel in Michigan, April 1991.

14. John Chubb, "Institutions, the Economy, and the Dynamics of State Elections," *American Political Science Review* 82 (March 1988): 133–54, at p. 151.

15. Ibid.

16. Samuel Peltzman, "Economic Conditions and Gubernatorial Elections," in Papers and Proceedings of the 99th Annual Meeting of the American Economics Association, *American Economic Review* 77 (May 1987): 293–97.

17. Chubb, "Institutions."

18. See, e.g., Cletus C. Coughlin and Thomas B. Mandelbaum, "Have Federal Spending and Taxation Contributed to the Divergence in State Per Capita Incomes in the 1980s?" *Federal Reserve Bank of St. Louis* 71 (July/August 1989): 29–42; L. Ray Cadwell and R. Lynn Ritenoure, "Recent Regional Growth Patterns: More Inequality," *Economic Development Quarterly* (August 1987): 240–48.

APPENDIX A

1. See, e.g., Thomas R. Dye, "Taxing, Spending and Economic Growth in the American States," *Journal of Politics* 42 (1980): 1085–1107; Paul Brace, "Isolating the Economies of States," *American Politics Quarterly* 17 (August 1989): 256–76; Brace, "The Changing Context of State Political Economy," *Journal of Politics* 53 (May 1991): 297–317; Rebecca Hendrick and James C. Garand, "Variations in State Economic Growth: Decomposing State, Regional and National Effects," *Journal of Politics* 53 (November 1991): 1093–1110; Mancur Olson, *The Rise and Decline of Nations* (New Haven: Yale University Press, 1982).

2. Robert H. Bates, ed., *Toward a Political Economy of Development: A Rational Choice Perspective* (Berkeley: University of California Press, 1988), 239.

3. Dan Usher, *The Measurement of Economic Growth* (New York: Columbia University Press, 1980); see also Bryan Jones, "Public Policies and Economic Growth in the American States," *Journal of Politics* 52 (February 1990): 219–33.

4. See E. F. Denison, "Welfare Measurement and the GNP," *Survey of Current Business* (1971): 1–9; Arthur M. Okun, "Should the GNP Measure Social Welfare?" *The Brookings Bulletin* 8 (Summer 1971): 4–7; F. T. Jusler, "A Frame-

work for the Measurement of Economic and Social Performance," in *The Measurement of Economic and Social Performance*, ed. M. Moss (Washington, D.C.: National Bureau of Economic Research, 1973): 25–84.

5. Usher, *Measurement*.

6. Joseph Schlesinger, "The Politics of the Executive," in *Politics in the American States*, ed. Herbert Jacobs and Kenneth N. Vines (Boston: Little, Brown, 1965).

7. Ibid., 2d ed. (1971).

8. Sarah McCalley Morehouse, *State Politics, Parties, and Policy* (New York: Holt, Rinehart, and Winston, 1981).

9. Keith Mueller, "Explaining Variation and Change in Gubernatorial Powers, 1960–1982." *Western Political Quarterly* 38 (1985): 424–31.

APPENDIX B

1. James A. Stimson, "Regression in Space and Time: A Statistical Essay," *American Journal of Political Science* 29 (November 1985): 914–47.

2. Paul E. Peterson and Mark Rom, "American Federalism, Welfare Policy, and Residential Choices," *American Political Science Review* 83 (1989): 711–28; Brace, "Changing Context" and "Isolating Economies"; Brace and Youssef Cohen, "How Much Do Interest Groups Influence State Economic Growth?" *American Political Science Review* 83 (December 1989): 1297–1308.

3. Jan Kmenta, *Elements of Econometrics*, 2d ed. (New York: Macmillan, 1986).

INDEX

accountability, 122
Adkins v. Children's Hospital, 134
AFL-CIO, 64
aircraft, 40, 45
Alabama, 49, 70, 73
Albany, New York, 139
Albritton, Robert B., 135n.34
Alexander Grant Company, 56
Ambrosius, Margery M., xiv, 140n.6,
   141n.20, 144n.8
America West Airlines, 41
Anderson, Harry, 138n.5
Applebome, Peter, 138n.42
Appropriations Committee, 20, 21
Arab Oil Embargo, 46, 96
Arbingast, Stanley A., 137n.32
Arizona, 14, 113; compared to Michigan,
   56, 59; compared to New York, 62;
   compared to Texas, 48–52;
   contemporary political economic
   conditions, 39–42; defense
   expenditures in, 97–98; economic
   development policies, 91–92;
   employment growth, 73; energy
   resources, 96; general policy liberalism
   score, 133n.40; governor's power, 88–
   90; growth in value added by
   manufacturing, 76, 78; investment
   expenditures in, 94; legislative
   resources, 90; personal income growth
   in, 70, 72; political economic history,
   33–39; Senate, 37, 41; taxation in, 91–
   93; unionization in, 97
Arizona Economic Council, 42
Arkansas, 66, 70, 76
Articles of Confederation, 17

Asia, 49
Austria, 9
automobile, 52–58, 72
Axelrod, Robert, 12, 133n.36

Babbitt, Bruce, 33
Bachelor, Lynn W., 9, 133n.31
bankruptcies, 137
Barker, Michael, 141n.19
Bartik, Timothy, 11, 26, 133n.35,
   135n.42, 140n.3, 142n.35
Bates, Robert H., 145n.2
Baumann, Philip, 144n.8
"beggar thy neighbor" development
   strategies, 13, 118
Beyle, Thad, 26, 135n.43, 140n.4
Bierman, Wallace W., 138n.6
Bisbee Workman's Loyalty League, 35
Blanchard, James, 57–58, 121
Bleany, Michael, 132n.12, 133n.28
Booth, Douglas E., 134n.2
Boston, Massachusetts, 49
Bowman, Ann O'M., 89, 90, 140n.15
Brierly, Alan, 145n.8
Briggs and Stratton, 53
Brown, Charles, 142n.7
Browne, Lynn, 26, 135n.37
Bryce, James, 23, 135n.27
Buchanan, James, 6, 8, 132n.17, 133n.26
Building a New American State, 21,
   135n.24

California, 23, 34, 36, 39, 45
Cameron, David, 142n.30
Campbell, Alan K., 26, 135n.35
capitalist, 142

Carey, Hugh, 63
Castles, F., 142n.30
"catallaxy," 5
Center for Industrial Innovation (New York), 63
Centers for Advanced Technology (New York), 63
Chance Vaught Aircraft, 45
Chicago, Illinois, 52
Chicago, Milwaukee and Saint Paul Railroad Co. v. Minnesota, 21
Choi, Kwang, 144n.8
Chubb, John, 122, 145nn.14, 17
Circle K, 42
Civil War, 18–20, 22, 43, 44
Clarke, Marianne C., 143n.43
Clinton, William, 66
Cobb, James, 25, 135n.33, 137n.36
Cohen, Youssef, xiv, 131n.4, 144n.8, 146n.11
Colander, D., 132n.16
Cold War, 115
Colorado, xiv, 70
Compendium of State Government Finance, 126
Congress, 21, 22
Conlan, Charles F., 135n.35
Connecticut, 70, 73, 76
Cooke, Jacob E., 134n.5
Corpus Christi Naval Air Station, 45
Coughlin, Cletus, 132n.7
Crash of 1929, 61
cross-national context, 95, 96, 114
Cumberland Road, 17
Cuomo, Mario, 63, 64

Dallas, Texas, 45, 65
Dean, James, 7, 132n.23, 133n.30
debt, 9, 20, 61
Delaware, 75, 76
demand-side approach, 28, 29, 44
democracy, 8, 53
Democratic party, 36, 37, 54, 57, 63, 95; control, 101–6, 108, 109
Denison, E. F., 145n.4
Department of Commerce (New York), 61, 64
Department of Economic Development (New York), 64
Detroit, Michigan, 53, 55–57
development, xiv, 87–89, 100–118, 120–22; in Arizona, 34–40, 42, 48–50; economic theories of, 2–5, 7–8, 10–11; in Michigan, 52–59; national context and, 30; in New York, 59–65; open economies and, 10, 11, 13; policies, 91; in Texas, 43, 45, 47–50; in U.S. history, 17–20, 22, 26–28

discrimination, 23
distributional context, 5, 6, 95
distributive arena, 61
diversity, 14, 31, 32
Dubnick, Melvin, 143n.41
Dudley, Robert, xiv, 131n.4, 143n.41, 144n.8
Durbin-Watson, 101, 104–6, 108, 109, 129
Dye, Thomas, 141n.23, 142n.36, 144n.8, 145n.1

Eisenger, Peter, 27–29, 91, 111, 136nn.47, 50, 51, 54, 138n.7, 141n.21, 143n.47, 144n.5
energy: crisis, 46; measurement of, 127; resources, 96–97. *See also* oil
enterprise, 17, 18, 38, 60
Entrepreneurial and Small Business Commission (Michigan), 58
entrepreneurs, 9, 19, 53
Erie Canal, 19, 60
Erikson, Robert, 133nn.38, 39
Europe, 8, 16–17, 122
exogenous economic influences, 6, 10, 49, 103, 116–18
expenditures: defense, 45, 97–99, 101–6; federal, 38; governmental, 17–18, 24, 33, 57, 65; investment, 26, 60, 63, 94, 101–9, 114, 119
external economic forces, and growth, 10, 34, 42, 49–50, 59, 65, 116–18. *See also* exogenous economic influences

Fantus Company, 56
federalism, 10, 17, 99
Feiock, Richard C., 115, 144n.4, 145n.8
Fenno, Richard F., 20, 134n.18
Fisher, Ronald C., 12, 131n.2, 133n.37
Flint, Michigan, 53
Ford, Henry, 53
Fosler, R. Scott, 27, 29, 136nn.45, 53, 56, 138nn.1, 10, 12, 139n.1, 140n.3

Gallatin, Albert, 17, 134n.6
Garand, James, 145n.1
Garrett, Geoffrey, 142n.30
General Dynamics, 45
Georgia, 76
Gitelson, Alan, 131n.4, 143n.41
GLS-ARMA, 129
GNP (Gross National Product), 24
Goodrich, Carter, 134n.16
Gottlieb, Robert, 136n.3
governor: influence of, on economic development, 101, 121; Schlesinger index of power of, 89–90, 126. *See also* *names of individual governors*

Governor's Commission on Jobs and
  Economic Development (Michigan), 57
Governor's High Technology Task Force
  (Michigan), 56
Grady, Dennis, 140n.3
Granger cases, 21–23
Gray, Virginia, xiv, 135n.34, 138n.2,
  140n.10, 141n.24, 144n.8
Great Depression, xiv, 24, 48, 55, 61
Greyhound, 36
Gross, Harold T., 139n.24
Grumm, John, 140nn.13, 14
Gunn, L. Ray, 19, 20, 61, 139n.17

Hamilton, Alexander, 17, 134n.5
Hansen, Susan, 140n.3, 141n.19
Hartz, Louis, 19, 134n.15
Hayek, F., 5, 6, 132nn.13, 14
Hazleton, Jared E., 137n.31
Helms, L. Jay, 143n.2
Henton, Douglas C., 140n.9
Herzik, Erik, 26, 135n.43
Hibbs, Douglas, 142n.9
Hicks, Alexander, 142n.30
high-technology industries, 37–40, 56,
  123
Hinckley, Barbara, xiv
Hirsch, Barry T., 142n.34
Hirschman, Albert O., 16, 131n.3,
  133n.1
Hodgson, Geoff, 7, 132n.22
Holman, Richard L., 131n.1
House of Representatives, U.S., 20–21
Houston, Texas, 44, 45, 48, 55
Hrebenar, Ronald J., 136n.1
Hudson, William E., 140n.11
Hughes, Jonathan R. T., 40, 134n.11
Hughes Aircraft, 40
Hwang Sung-Don, 141n.24
Hyde, Mark S., 140n.11

IBM (International Business Machines),
  40
ideology, 14, 25, 95
Illinois, xv, 19, 21, 23
income, 24; per capita, 69–73, 75, 79–82,
  84–86, 99–105, 107–12, 125; personal,
  2, 37–38, 52, 59, 62, 65, 78, 114–23;
  redistribution, 13, 97; reversal of long-
  term trend in, 2; tax, 30, 47–48, 57
incorporation, 22, 100
Indiana, 19, 70, 140
individualism, 5, 34, 35, 38
Industrial Cooperation Council (New
  York), 63, 64
Industrial Revolution, 61
industries, 19, 28–29, 36–40, 43–48, 52–
  59, 63–65

inefficiencies, 5, 6
inequality, 5, 23
inertia, 100, 101, 104–9, 111
infrastructure, 13, 30–31, 46, 93–94, 107,
  118–19
innovation, 24, 53, 121–23; in Michigan,
  121; in New York, 121; policy
  innovation, 89; technological, 75, 106,
  119
interest groups, 6, 38, 95
internal improvements, 17, 18, 20
interstate commerce, 21–23
Interstate Commerce Act, 22
Interstate Commerce Commission, 22,
  23
interstate competition, 11
intervention, 5, 65, 113–16, 122–23; in
  Arizona, 40, 42; federal, 2–3, 17, 19–
  22, 23–34; in Michigan, 53, 55, 57, 59;
  in New York, 60–61, 63; state, 3, 18,
  22–23, 24–25, 28–32, 116; in Texas, 47
interventionist strategies, 9, 10, 13–14,
  54, 65, 112–14
investment. *See* expenditures
Iowa, 23, 69, 70
Ivey, Mark, 138n.44

Jackman, John E., 114, 142nn.31, 32,
  143n.1
Jackson, John E., 18, 52, 53, 58, 88–89,
  138n.1, 139n.1, 140nn.3, 12
Jacobs, Herbert, 135nn.34, 43, 137n.38,
  138n.2, 140n.5, 146n.6
Japan, 9, 56, 58, 122
Jefferson, Thomas, 17
Job Development Authority (New York),
  61
jobs, 52, 54–55, 64–65, 67, 103, 105–7,
  111–12, 115; high-technology, 37; low-
  paying, 41, 49. *See also* employment
Johnson, E. A., 134n.14
Johnson, Lyndon Baines, 97
Jones, Bryan, xiv, 9, 93, 133n.31,
  141n.24, 145n.3
Jusler, F. T., 145n.4

Kansas, 23, 73
Kearny, Richard C., 89, 90, 140n.15
Keech, William, xiv
Kelly Field, 45
Kenski, Henry, 143n.43
Keynes, John Maynard, 8, 133n.25
Kimmel, Lewis, 134n.10
King, Anthony, 87, 139 (chap. 6
  epigraph)
Klingman, David, 133n.40
Kmenta, Jan, 146n.12
Koretz, Gene, 145n.12

laissez faire, 7, 18, 20–25, 30, 38, 39
Lammers, William W., 133n.40
Lampe, David, 3, 132n.10, 136n.46
Landry, Larry, 136n.13, 140n.3
Lange, Peter, 142n.30
Lansing, Michigan, 53
lateral competition, 11, 13, 118, 120
leadership, 46, 55, 65, 88, 122
legislature, 21–23, 36–38, 45–47, 54–57,
    61–65, 89, 95, 127
Leontif, Wasily, 142n.12
Letwin, William, 134n.12
Lindblom, Charles, 9, 133n.29
Lochner v. New York, 134
Los Angeles, California, 36
Louisiana, 70, 75–76
Lowery, David, xiv, 144n.8
Luke Air Force Base, 36

Magid, Alvin, 63, 139n.19
management, 1, 35, 53, 88, 121
Mandelbaum, Thomas B., 132, 145
manufacturing, 37; in Arizona, 40; in
    Michigan, 52–53, 56, 58–59; in New
    York, 59–65; state government's role
    in stimulating, 18–19, 114–15; in
    Texas, 45–46; value added by, 69, 76–
    79, 84–87, 100, 107–12, 125
market-oriented approaches to growth,
    4–10
Maryland, 144
Mason, Bruce, 136n.1
Massachusetts, 3, 70
Mauro, Frank J., 139n.18
McGuire, Therese, 141n.24, 143n.2
McHone, W. Warren, 26, 135n.40
McPheters, Lee R., 137n.15
Mecham, Evan, 41
Medoff, James, 142n.37
methodology, xiv, 69, 128–29
Mexico, 40, 76
Michigan: contemporary political
    economic conditions, 62–65; defense
    expenditures in, 97–98; economic
    development policies in, 91–93;
    energy resources, 96; general policy
    liberalism score, 133n.40; governor's
    power in, 88–90; investment
    expenditures in, 94; legislative
    resources in, 90; and personal income,
    72; political economic history, 51–59;
    taxation in, 93; unionization in, 97;
    and value added by manufacturing,
    78
Michigan Manufacturing Association, 56
migration, 39, 42, 45, 48, 50, 75, 104
military, economic influence of, 35–36,
    38, 45, 97, 102–3

Miller, Nathan, 138n.15
Milliken, William, 54, 56–59
mining, 35–37
Minnesota, 21, 23
Mississippi Valley, 23
Missouri, 23, 73
Mollenkopf, John H., 10, 133n.32
Montana, 76
Morehouse, Sarah McCally, 47, 136n.8,
    138n.39, 140n.5, 146n.8
Moss, M., 146n.4
Motorola, 36
Mucciaroni, Gary, xiv, 142n.41, 143n.44
Mueller, Denis, 132n.23, 144n.5
Mueller, Keith, 137n.38, 140n.5, 146n.9
Munn v. Illinois, 134n.21

Nash, Gerald D., 134n.13
Nathan, Richard P., 131n.4, 143n.42
national context, 16–19, 21–27, 29–31,
    79, 84, 96, 100, 113
National Turnpike, 17
national-level economic influences, 70,
    76, 78–79, 81–85, 108, 112, 115–16
Nebraska, 73
neoclassical economic theory, 5–7, 9, 116
New Deal, 24, 54
New Hampshire, 70
New Jersey, 70, 73
New Mexico, 76
New York, xiv, 14; contemporary
    political economic conditions, 62–65;
    defense expenditures in, 97–98;
    economic development policies in, 91–
    92; employment growth, 73; energy
    resources, 96; general policy liberalism
    index in, 133n.40; governor's power
    in, 88–90; growth in value added by
    manufacturing, 76, 78; investment
    expenditures in, 94; legislative
    resources, 90; personal income growth
    in, 70, 73; political economic history,
    19–20, 42, 59–62; taxation in, 91–93;
    unionization in, 97
New York State Science and Technology
    Foundation, 63
Newman, Stephen, 132n.19
Niskanen, William, 132n.17
North Dakota, 69
Norway, 9

O'Driscoll, Gerald P., 137n.15
Ohio, 17, 19
oil: crisis of 1973, 81, 102–3; importance
    of, to Texas economy, 44–50, 93–94,
    96–107; and the Michigan economy,
    55–56. *See also* energy; Persian Gulf
    Crisis

Oklahoma, 69, 76
Okun, Arthur, 145n.4
Old South, New South, 25, 137n.30
Olds, Ransom, 53
OLS (Ordinary Least Squares), 128, 129
Olson, Mancur, 6, 7, 95, 117, 131n.1, 141n.28, 144n.8
Osborne, David, 3, 38, 132n.8, 136n.9, 140n.3

Panic of 1837, 20
parties, political: in Arizona, 36–37, 42; and economic performance, 7, 32, 87–114; measurement, 126; in Michigan, 54, in Texas, 46
Path to Prosperity: The Findings and Recommendations of the Task Force for a Long Term Economic Strategy for Michigan, 58, 138 (chap. 4 epigraph), 139nn.4, 11, 143n.4, 144n.3
Patterson, Tom, 41
payrolls, 45, 137
Peirce, Neil R., 139n.23
Peltzman, Samuel, 121, 145n.16
Pencak, William, 134n.17, 139n.17
Pennsylvania, 19, 69, 73
Perry, David C., 134n.2
Persian Gulf Crisis, 50
Peterson, Paul, 10, 93, 117, 118, 133n.33, 141n.22, 144n.6, 146n.11
petroleum, 44, 45
philosophy, 7, 17, 35
Phoenix, Arizona, 35, 36, 39, 40
Plaut, Thomas, 26, 135n.38, 141n.19
Pluta, Joseph, 26, 135n.38, 141n.19
Polanyi, Karl, 7, 132n.21
pooled cross-sectional time series, 80, 100
Premus, Robert, 136n.52
probusiness orientations, 33, 34, 36–38, 47–49, 113
professionalism, 30, 88–89, 101, 103
Pryor, Frederick L., 144n.8

Railroad and Commerce Commission (Illinois), 23
railroads, 22, 23, 52
Reagan, Ronald, and changes in state-federal relations, 1–2, 31, 82–87, 99, 103, 112–13
recession, 1, 19, 29, 55, 62, 79, 121
recovery, 3, 29, 39, 44, 50, 57, 59, 62
Rees, Albert, 142n.35
Report on Manufactures (Hamilton), 17
Republican party, 36, 37, 41, 42, 54, 95; control, 101–6, 108, 109
responsiveness, 67, 70, 72, 75, 78, 114
Rex, Tom R., 138n.43

Rhode Island, 69, 70, 75, 89
Rich, Robert, xv
Richardson, Dennis, 137n.32
Right-to-Work law (Arizona), 38
Rise and Decline of Nations, xiv, 6, 95, 117, 131n.1, 139n.1, 141n.28, 144n.7, 145n.1
Ritenoure, R. Lynn, 132n.7, 145n.18
Rodriguez, Louis J., 137n.31
Rom, Mark C., 146n.11
Romney, George, 54
Roosevelt, Franklin, 24
Roosevelt, Theodore, 135n.28
Rosenthal, Alan, 140n.4
Rostow, Walter, 134n.2
Roth, Paul F., 48
Russett, Bruce, 97, 98, 142n.40
rustbelt, 52, 70, 89, 97

Sabato, Larry, 140n.7
Sankey, Bruce, 137nn.18, 20
Schlesinger, Arthur M., Jr., 134nn.7, 19
Schlesinger, Joseph A., 140n.5, 146n.6
Schmenner, Roger, 26, 135n.41
Schoolman, Morton, 139n.19
Senate, U.S., 21, 22
Sharkansky, Ira, 140n.13
short-term approach, 58, 62, 118, 119
Silicon Valley, 106
Site Selection Handbook, 91, 92, 126
Skoro, Charles L., 138n.9
Skowronek, Stephen, 21, 22, 134n.24, 135nn.24, 26
Smith, Adam, 4, 5, 7, 132n.11
South Carolina, 19, 49, 70
South Dakota, 69, 70
Southwestern Bell Telephone Company, 48
Spindletop, Texas, 44
"spontaneous order," 5
Srinivasan, T. N., 7, 132n.20
stagnation, 3, 6, 14, 64, 108
Standard Oil Company, 44
state capacity, 14–32, 112
state-level economic activities, 25–32, 67, 72–86, 97–99, 108–9, 115–17, 121–23, 128
Statistical Abstract of the United States, 93, 94, 126, 127, 137n.33
Stimson, James, 128, 146n.10
Stryk, R., 135n.36
subsidy, 21, 91
sunbelt, 14, 33, 52, 65, 70, 89, 91, 97
supply-side approach, 27–29, 44
Supreme Court, U.S., 21–23
Suro, Robert, 136 (chap. 3 epigraph), 137n.34, 138n.4
Survey of Current Business, 125

Swank, Duane, 142n.30
Sweden, 9
Switzerland, 9
Symington, Fife, 41–42

taxation: economic effects of, 91–93, 114, 118–22; measurement, 126; tax preferences, 62
technologies, 12, 42, 58, 123
Tese, Vincent, 64
Texas, 14, 33, 34, 40; compared to Arizona, 40, 48–50; compared to New York, 59, 65; contemporary political economic conditions, 47; economic development policies in, 91–92; employment growth, 72; energy resources, 96; governor's power in, 88–91; growth in value added by manufacturing, 76; investment expenditures in, 94; legislative resources in, 90; personal income growth in, 70; political economic history, 43–47; taxation in, 91–93
Therborn, Goran, 9, 133n.27
Thomas, Clive, 136n.1
Tiebout, Charles, 10, 11, 119, 133n.34, 145n.11
timber, 52
training, 11, 28, 42, 62–64, 115
transportation, 19, 37, 52, 60
Tucson, Arizona, 39, 40
Tullock, Gordon, 132

unemployment, 9, 24; in Arizona, 39, 41; in Michigan, 55, 72; in New York, 59, 64
unions: in Arizona, 35; economic effects of, 97; measurement, 127; in Michigan, 56; in Texas, 43
United Auto Workers, 53
unskilled workforce, 43, 49

Urban Job Incentive Program (New York), 62
Usher, Dan, 125, 145n.3, 146n.5
Utah, 136

Van Horn, Carl, 88, 131n.4, 135n.32, 139n.2
Vaughn, R. J., 141n.19
Vedder, Richard K., 26, 135n.39
Vedlitz, Arnold, 141n.22
Vermont, 73, 76
Vines, Kenneth, 137n.38, 138n.2, 140nn.5, 10, 146n.6
Virginia, 19

Wagner, Richard E., 8, 132n.17, 133n.26
Waldhorn, Steven A., 140nn.3, 9
Ward, Daniel, 140n.13
Warren, Charles R., 140n.3
Warren, Ronald S., 142n.35
Wasylenko, Michael, 141n.24, 143n.2
Watkins, Alfred J., 134n.2
Ways and Means Committee, 20
Webber, Carolyn, 24, 134n.8, 135n.30
Weinstein, Bernard, 65, 139n.24
White, Will, xv
Whitely, Paul, 142n.38
Wildavsky, Aaron, 24, 134n.8, 135n.30
Williams, Bruce A., 135n.34
Wilson, Carter, 133n.31
Wilson, Woodrow, 24, 135n.29
Wisconsin, 23
Wright, Gavin, 25, 43, 137n.30
Wright, Gerald, 133nn.38, 39
Wyoming, 70, 76

Yago, Glenn, 139n.18
Young, Jacob, 138n.5

Zeigler, Harmon, 140n.10
zero-sum game, 11, 12

DATE DUE

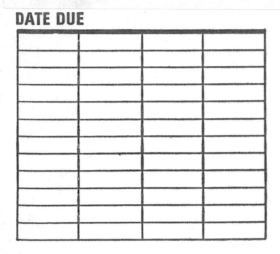

DEMCO